Mike McGrath

HTML5

in
easy steps

Second Edition

Covers the new HTML 5.1 W3C R

D1119466

In easy steps is an imprint of In Easy Steps Limited
16 Hamilton Terrace · Holly Walk · Leamington Spa
Warwickshire · United Kingdom · CV32 4LY
www.ineasysteps.com

Second Edition

Notice of Liability
Every effort has been made to ensure that this book contains accurate
and current information. However, In Easy Steps Limited and the
author shall not be liable for any loss or damage suffered by readers
as a result of any information contained herein.

Trademarks
All trademarks are acknowledged as belonging to their respective
companies.

In Easy Steps Limited supports The Forest Stewardship Council (FSC),
the leading international forest certification organization. All our titles
that are printed on Greenpeace approved FSC certified paper carry the
FSC logo.

MIX
Paper from
responsible sources
FSC® C020837

Printed and bound in the United Kingdom

ISBN 978-1-84078-754-2

Contents

1 Getting started 9

Introducing HTML5 10
Addressing web pages 12
Defining document structure 14
Creating a document 16
Validating documents 18
Employing an HTML editor 20
Summary 22

2 Providing page information 23

Bestowing a title 24
Specifying a character set 26
Refreshing the page 28
Describing the document 30
Incorporating scripts 32
Incorporating style sheets 34
Linking more resources 36
Summary 38

3 Creating body content 39

Working the body 40
Inserting paragraphs 42
Including quotations 44
Emphasizing text 46
Reading the small print 48
Marking text 50
Keeping preformatted text 52
Modifying text 54
Including code in text 56
Giving tooltip advice 58
Adding images 60
Directing languages 62
Summary 64

4 Inserting hyperlinks 65

Creating hyperlinks 66
Accessing links via keys 68
Linking to page fragments 70
Linking to protocols 72
Using images as hyperlinks 74
Producing image map links 76
Generating popups 78
Summary 80

5 Arranging content sections 81

Proclaiming headings 82
Grouping headers 84
Providing navigation 86
Writing articles 88
Standing aside 90
Footing the page 92
Positioning content 94
Denying anonymity 96
Summary 98

6 Writing lists and tables 99

Creating unordered lists 100
Creating ordered lists 102
Creating definition lists 104
Producing a simple table 106
Spanning cells over rows 108
Spanning cells across columns 110
Adding a header and footer 112
Aligning cell content 114
Grouping columns 116
Setting column widths 118
Utilizing templates 120
Summary 122

7 Embedding media content 123

Referencing figures 124
Selecting pictures 126
Embedding objects 128
Specifying parameters 130
Embedding in frames 132
Embedding plugin movies 134
Embedding audio 136
Embedding video 138
Indicating progress 140
Summary 142

8 Building input forms 143

Submitting forms 144
Gathering text input 146
Controlling input type 148
Providing text areas 150
Checking boxes 152
Choosing radio buttons 154
Selecting options 156
Utilizing hidden data 158
Pushing buttons 160
Using images for submission 162
Adding logos to buttons 164
Labeling form controls 166
Listing data options 168
Uploading files 170
Summary 172

9   Painting on canvas   173

Generating a canvas   174
Painting shapes   176
Stroking borders   178
Filling options   180
Writing text   182
Drawing lines   184
Swerving curves   186
Translating coordinates   188
Transforming shapes   190
Animating the canvas   192
Summary   194

10   Employing APIs   195

Measuring fractions   196
Dragging and dropping objects   198
Manipulating pixels   200
Storing user data   202
Editing live content   204
Cross-document messaging   206
Pinpointing the user   208
Summary   210

+   Handy reference   211

Global HTML5 attributes   212
HTML5 element tags   214
CSS properties & values   232

Index   233

The creation of this book has been for me, Mike McGrath, an exciting opportunity to discover how the latest specification of HTML5 can be implemented in today's web browsers. Whereas my previous books on web page markup described the HTML 4.01 and HTML 5.0 specifications, it has been fascinating to see how the HTML 5.1 specifications are supported in Microsoft Edge, Internet Explorer, Firefox, Google Chrome, Safari, and Opera web browsers.

The "Handy Reference" section at the end of the book lists the HTML5 tags and attributes that are included in the HTML 5.1 specifications. All the examples I have given in this book demonstrate HTML5 features that are supported by leading web browsers, and the screenshots illustrate the actual results produced by the listed code. I truly believe that now, more than ever, authors can integrate HTML5 content markup, JavaScript functionality, and CSS presentation, to produce stunning interactive web pages.

Conventions in this book

In order to clarify the code listed in the steps given in each example I have adopted certain colorization conventions. Those parts of the HTML language itself are colored blue, like this:

```
<html>
```

Values assigned to HTML attributes are colored red, like this:

```
<html lang="en">
```

Literal content that is marked up by HTML tags is colored black, like this:

```
<title>HTML5 in easy steps</title>
```

Similarly, for style sheet code listed in the steps, those parts of the CSS language itself are colored blue and values assigned to properties are colored red, like this:

```
h1       { color : red ; background : yellow ; }
```

Additionally, in order to identify each source code file described in the steps, a colored icon and the file name appears in the margin alongside the steps, such as these:

page.html   style.css   script.js   vector.svg   embed.pdf   audio.ogg   video.mp4

Grabbing the source code

For convenience I have placed all the source code files and associated files featured in this book into a single ZIP archive file, which you can obtain by following these easy steps:

1 Browse to **www.ineasysteps.com** then navigate to Free Resources and choose the Downloads section

2 Find HTML5 in easy steps, 2nd edition in the list, then click on the hyperlink entitled All Code Examples to download the archive

3 Now, extract the archive contents to any convenient location on your computer

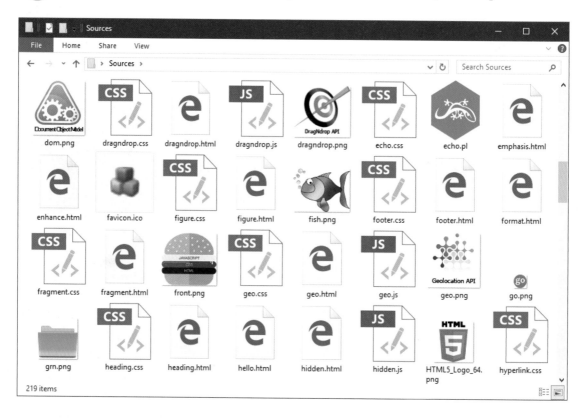

Undoubtedly, HTML5 provides significant new creative possibilities in web page authoring – as I hope my examples demonstrate. I sincerely hope you enjoy discovering how HTML5 can be used to create stunning interactive web pages in today's latest web browsers as much as I did in writing this book.

Mike McGrath

1 Getting started

Welcome to the exciting world of the HTML5 web. This chapter introduces HTML5 and demonstrates how to create a "barebones" valid HTML5 document.

10 Introducing HTML5

12 Addressing web pages

14 Defining document structure

16 Creating a document

18 Validating documents

20 Employing an HTML editor

22 Summary

Introducing HTML5

Historically, the desire to have text printed in specific formats meant that original manuscripts were "marked up" with annotation to indicate to the book-printer how the author would like sections of text laid out. This annotation had to be concise and needed to be easily understood by both the printer and the author. A series of commonly recognized abbreviations therefore formed the basis of a standard markup language.

HyperText Markup Language (HTML) is a modern standard markup language that uses common abbreviations called "tags" to indicate to the web browser how the author would like to have sections of a web page laid out. It was first devised in March 1989 by British physicist Tim Berners-Lee at CERN in Switzerland (the European organization for nuclear research) to share all computer-stored information between the CERN physicists. Berners-Lee created a text browser to transfer information over the internet using hypertext to provide point-and-click navigation. In May 1990 this system was named the World Wide Web, and was enhanced in 1993 when college student Marc Andreessen added an image tag. Now that HTML could display both text and images, the World Wide Web quickly became hugely popular.

Sir Tim Berners-Lee, creator of the World Wide Web.

As various web browsers were developed, their makers began to add individual proprietary tags – effectively creating their own versions of HTML! The World Wide Web Consortium (W3C) standards organization recognized the danger that HTML could become fragmented, so they created a standard specification to which all web browsers should adhere. This successfully encouraged the browser makers to support the standard tags. The W3C's HTML specification was continually revised to introduce new features until the publication of HTML version 4.01 at the turn of the century. At that time the W3C also published a specification for XHTML (eXtensible HTML), which strictly required all code to be "well-formed", to comply with the rules of eXtensible Markup Language (XML). This attempt to coerce web authors into adopting rigorous syntax, as Berners-Lee admits, did not work. So the W3C returned to HTML and finally produced a specification for version 5 in October 2014. This was updated on November 1, 2016 to version 5.1. The supported features of the HTML 5.1 version are described and demonstrated in this book, where it is generically referred to as "HTML5" or just plain "HTML".

The W3C is the recognized body that oversees the HTML standard and other standards on the web. See the latest developments on their informative website at **www.w3.org**

What's new in HTML5?

Placing great emphasis on backward compatibility, HTML5 is largely a superset of the previous versions, but it introduces some new features that let authors create more meaningful web pages:

- **<main>** – a structural element to contain the main content
- **<article>** – a structural element to contain stand-alone items of content, such as a self-contained topic
- **<section>** – a structural element to group together associated content, such as articles related to a common topic
- **<aside>** – a structural element to contain related content
- **<figure>**, **<figcaption>** – structural elements to contain stand-alone illustrations, diagrams, or photos for reference
- **<header>** – a structural element to contain page header content, such as a title, logo, and navigation
- **<footer>** – a structural element to contain page footer content, such as copyright information and contact details
- **<ruby>**, **<rt>**, and **<rp>** – semantic elements to indicate pronunciation for East Asian languages, such as Japanese
- **<audio>**, **<video>**, and **<source>** – embedding elements to incorporate audio and video media, such as MP3 music files
- **<embed>** – an embedding element to incorporate media that <u>does</u> require an external plug-in, such as movies in SWF format
- **<canvas>** – an embedding element to create an area in which to dynamically draw bitmap graphics, such as graphs
- **<details>**, **<summary>** – interactive elements to contain additional information that users can choose to read
- **<menu>**, **<menuitem>** – elements to add functionality to the web browser's context menu

Drawing on the area provided by the **<canvas>** element is accomplished exclusively using JavaScript and the Canvas 2D API (Application Programming Interface). HTML5 also includes Drag and Drop, Web Storage, and Messaging APIs with which JavaScript can provide dynamic web page functionality.

Much effort has been made in HTML5 so that it does not "break the web" – by continuing to define how browsers should deal with legacy markup code.

HTML5 finally brings intrinsic support for audio and video content with codec support built into the browsers.

The New icon pictured above indicates new features introduced in the very latest W3C HTML 5.1 specifications.

Addressing web pages

The World Wide Web comprises a series of large-capacity computers, known as "web servers", which are connected to the internet via telephone lines and satellites. The web servers each use the HyperText Transfer Protocol (HTTP) as a common communication standard to allow any computer connected to any web server to access files across the web.

HTML web pages are merely plain text files that have been saved with a ".htm" or ".html" file extension, such as **index.html**.

In order to access a file across the web, its web address must be entered into the address field of the web browser. The web address is formally known as its "Uniform Resource Locator" (URL) and typically has three parts:

- **Protocol** – any URL using the HTTP protocol begins by specifying the protocol as **http://** or secure **https://**
- **Domain** – the host name of the computer from which the file can be downloaded. For instance, **www.example.com**
- **Path** – the virtual path to the file on the named domain, including any parent directory names where applicable. For instance, **/htdocs/index.html**

A URL describing the location of a file by protocol, domain, and path is stating its "absolute address". So the absolute address of the file described by the protocol, domain, and path components above is **http://www.example.com/htdocs/index.html**

Code contained within an HTML web page can reference other HTML files in any domain by their absolute address. HTML files resident within the same domain can also be referenced more simply by their "relative address", which means that files located within the same directory can be referenced just by their file name. For instance, a file named "adjacent.html" located in the same directory can be referenced simply as **adjacent.html**.

Additionally, a relative address can reference a file within the parent directory by prefixing its name with "../". For instance, a file named "higher.html" in the parent directory can be referenced from the current directory as **../higher.html**.

Beware

A web page address (URL) cannot contain any blank spaces.

Hot tip

Where an address states only the HTTP protocol and a domain name, most web servers are configured to seek a file named **index.html** in their default directory.

How do web servers work?

When you enter a URL into the browser address field, the browser first examines the protocol. Where the protocol is specified as HTTP, or assumed to be HTTP if unspecified, the browser recognizes that a file is being sought from a web server. It then contacts a Domain Name Server (DNS) to look up the numerical Internet Protocol (IP) address of the specified domain name. Next, a connection is established with the web server at that IP address to request the file at the specified path. When the file is successfully located it is copied back to the browser, otherwise the web server sends an error code, such as "404 – Page Not Found".

The Domain Name Server is typically run by your Internet Service Provider or by your company.

A successful response sends HTTP headers to the web browser, describing the nature of the response, along with a copy of the requested file. The HTTP headers are not normally visible but can be examined using various development tools, such as the F12 Developer Tools feature in the Microsoft Edge web browser:

Notice in the headers that the Content-Type is "text/html" – the MIME type used by all web servers to describe plain text HTML files.

Defining document structure

The structure of an HTML5 document has these three parts:

- **Document type declaration** – declaring precisely which version of HTML is used to mark up the document
- **Head section** – providing descriptive data about the document itself, such as the document's title and the character set used
- **Body section** – containing the content that is to appear when the document gets loaded into a web browser

Document type declaration

The document type declaration must appear at the start of the first line of every HTML5 document to ensure the web browser will "render" (display) the document in "Standards Mode" – following the HTML5 specifications. The document type declaration tag for all HTML5 documents looks like this:

```
<!DOCTYPE HTML>
```

It is important to note that HTML5 is not a case-sensitive language – so the document type declaration tag, and all other tags, may alternatively be written in any combination of uppercase and lowercase characters. For example, the following are all valid:

```
<!DOCTYPE html>
```

```
<!Doctype Html>
```

```
<!doctype html>
```

The choice of capitalization is yours, but it is recommended you adhere consistently to whichever style you choose. The document type declaration tag capitalization style favored throughout this book uses all uppercase to emphasize its prominence as the very first tag on each page – but all other tags are in all lowercase.

Those familiar with previous versions of HTML may be surprised at the simplicity of the HTML5 document type declaration. In fact, the document type declaration in earlier versions was not actually part of the HTML language – so required lengthy references to schema documents. By contrast, the HTML5 document type declaration is an intrinsic part of HTML itself.

The document type declaration in earlier versions of HTML was part of the Standard Generalized Markup Language (SGML) from which HTML is derived.

The entire document head section and body section can be enclosed within a pair of **<html>** **</html>** tags to contain the rest of the document. The HTML5 specification actually states that these are optional, but it is logical to provide a single "root" element. Most HTML tags are used in pairs like this to act as "containers" with the syntax **< *tagname* > *data* </ *tagname* >**.

Head section

The document's head section begins with an HTML opening **<head>** tag and ends with a corresponding closing **</head>** tag. Data describing the document can be added later between these two tags to complete the HTML document's head section.

Body section

The document's body section begins with an HTML opening **<body>** tag and ends with a corresponding closing **</body>** tag. Data content to appear in the browser can be added later between these two tags to complete the HTML document's body section.

Code comments

Comments can be added at any point within both the head and body sections between a pair of **<!--** and **-->** tags. Anything that appears between the comment tags is ignored by the browser.

Fundamental structure

So, the markup tags that create the fundamental structure of every HTML5 document look like this:

```
<!DOCTYPE HTML>

<html>
 <head>
  <!-- Data describing the document to be added here -->
 </head>

 <body>
  <!-- Data content to appear in the browser to be added here -->
 </body>

</html>
```

Hot tip

An HTML "element" is any matching pair of opening and closing tags, or any single tag not requiring a closing tag – as described in the HTML5 element tags list on the inside front cover of this book.

Hot tip

The "invisible" characters that represent tabs, newlines, carriage returns, and spaces are collectively known as "whitespace". They may optionally be used to inset the tags for clarity.

The **<meta>** tag is a single tag – it does not have a matching closing tag. See the element tags list on the inside front cover of this book to find other single tags.

HTML

hello.html

Beware

IHTML documents should not be created in word processors, such as MS Word, as they include additional information in their file formats.

Creating a document

The fundamental HTML5 document structure, described on page 15, can be used to create a simple HTML5 document in any plain text editor – such as Windows' Notepad application. In order to create a valid "barebones" HTML5 document, information must first be added defining the document's primary written language, its character encoding format, and its title.

The document's primary language is defined by assigning a standard language code to a **lang** "attribute" within the opening **<html>** root tag. For the English language the code is **en**, so the complete opening root element looks like this: **<html lang="en">**.

The document's character encoding format is defined by assigning a standard character-set code to a **charset** attribute within a **<meta>** tag placed in the document's head section. The recommended encoding is the popular 8-bit Unicode Transformation Format for which the code is **UTF-8**, so the complete element looks like this: **<meta charset="UTF-8">**.

Finally, the document's title is defined by text between a pair of **<title>** **</title>** tags placed in the document's head section.

Follow these steps to create a valid "barebones" HTML5 document:

1 Launch your favorite plain text editor, then start a new document with the HTML5 document type declaration
<!DOCTYPE HTML>

2 Below the document type declaration, add a root element that defines the document's primary language as English
<html lang="en">
  <!-- Head and Body sections to be added here -->
</html>

3 Within the root element, insert a document head section
<head>
  <!-- Descriptive information to be added here -->
</head>

4 Within the head section, insert an element defining the document's encoding character set
<meta charset="UTF-8">

5 Next, within the head section, insert an element defining the document's title
`<title>Getting Started</title>`

6 After the head section, insert a document body section
```
<body>
 <!-- Actual document content to be added here -->
</body>
```

7 Within the body section, insert a size-one large heading
`<h1>Hello World!</h1>`

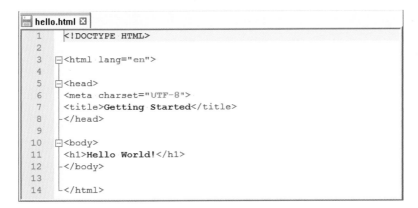

```
 hello.html
 1    <!DOCTYPE HTML>
 2
 3   <html lang="en">
 4
 5   <head>
 6    <meta charset="UTF-8">
 7    <title>Getting Started</title>
 8   </head>
 9
10   <body>
11    <h1>Hello World!</h1>
12   </body>
13
14   </html>
```

8 Save the document as "hello.html", setting the encoding to the popular "UTF-8" format

```
Encoding
   Encode in ANSI
 • Encode in UTF-8
   Encode in UTF-8-BOM
```

9 Now, open the HTML5 document in a modern web browser to see the title displayed on the title bar or tab, and the document content displayed as a large heading

Getting Started   ×   +

hello.html

Hello World!

Don't forget

The quotation marks around an attribute value are usually optional, but are required for multiple values. For consistency, attribute values in the examples throughout this book are all surrounded by quotation marks.

Beware

Windows' Notepad automatically adds a hidden "Byte Order Mark" (BOM) to the file, while other editors (such as Notepad++ shown here) allow this to be omitted. Notepad++ can be freely downloaded from **notepad-plus-plus.org**

Validating documents

The W3C's online HTML validator can be found at **validator.w3.org**

Just as text documents may contain spelling and grammar errors, HTML documents may contain various errors that prevent them from conforming to the specification rules. In order to verify that an HTML document does indeed conform to the rules of its specified document type declaration, it can be tested by a validator tool. Only HTML documents that pass the validation test successfully are sure to be valid documents.

Web browsers make no attempt at validation, so it is well worth verifying every HTML document with a validator tool before it is published, even when the content looks fine in your web browser. When the browser encounters HTML errors it will make a guess at what is intended – but different browsers can make different interpretations so may display the document incorrectly. Conversely, valid HTML documents should always appear correctly in any standards-compliant browser.

The World Wide Web Consortium (W3C) provides a free online validator tool that checks the syntax of web documents:

1 With an internet connection, open your web browser and navigate to the W3C Validator Tool at **validator.w3.org**, then click on the "Validate by File Upload" tab

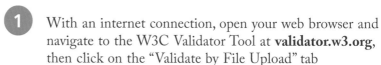

Other tabs in the validator allow you to enter the web address of an HTML document located on a web server to "Validate by URI" or copy and paste all code from a document to "Validate by Direct Input".

2 Click the "Browse" button, then navigate to the HTML document you wish to validate – once selected, its local path appears in the validator's "File" field

3 Next, click the validator's "Check" button to upload a copy of the HTML document and run the validation test – the results will then be displayed

The validator automatically detects the document's character set and HTML version.

If validation fails, the errors are listed so you may easily correct them. When validation succeeds, you may choose to include an icon at the end of the document demonstrating HTML5 support:

The HTML5 support logo is available in several sizes and formats – find more details online at w3.org/html/logo

Employing an HTML editor

HTML code can be created in any plain text editor that provides encoding in the recommended UTF-8 format. As long as the code in the new text file is saved with a file extension of ".html" or ".htm", an HTML document is created. This file can then be opened in any web browser, such as Microsoft Edge, to see how the HTML code is interpreted to "render" (display) the content on the screen.

Older web browsers, such as Internet Explorer 8 or earlier, will not fully recognize the modern HTML5 markup code. It is best, therefore, to view HTML5 web pages in the latest version of the Microsoft Edge, Internet Explorer, Firefox, Google Chrome, Opera, and Safari web browsers.

Some HTML authors prefer to use specialized HTML editors that colorize the various parts of the source code for greater clarity, and offer further features. Microsoft's Expression Web editor, shown below, is a popular choice for some HTML authors.

At the time of writing, Expression Web 4 is available free for download at **microsoft. com/en-us/download/ details.aspx?id=36179**

Beware

The Expression Web interface also allows web pages to be created visually by dragging components onto its Design window – but knowledge of HTML is often helpful in fine-tuning the web page.

20

The Split view in Expression Web provides a live preview of what the HTML document will look like in a web browser. Additionally, a built-in menu lets you quickly view the document in any web browser installed on your computer.

The W3C online validator tool can also be used to verify correct HTML code, along with Expression Web's Compatibility Checker tool.

Expression Web's "Compatibility Checker" tool lets you easily locate code errors that do not conform to the declared document type. Additionally, like other Microsoft development tools, the Expression Web editor has "IntelliSense", which identifies syntax errors live as you type the HTML code. This feature also provides context-sensitive menus that can insert HTML tags compatible with the current point in the document. For example, when you type a "<" in the head section, IntelliSense presents a list of tags that may be inserted at that point. After selecting a tag and typing a space, IntelliSense then presents a list of attributes that may be inserted within that tag.

By default, IntelliSense automatically inserts a matching closing tag, if appropriate, whenever you type an opening tag. Some authors dislike this ability, however, but the Expression Web options allow IntelliSense features to be turned on and off individually to customize the editor to your personal taste.

Expression Web also provides a customizable Code Snippet facility to quickly insert frequently used chunks of code – press **Ctrl** + **Enter** to see the Code Snippet list.

21

Summary

- The World Wide Web Consortium (W3C) is the recognized body that oversees standards on the web.

- HTML5 introduces intrinsic support for audio and video media content.

- JavaScript can draw on canvas areas and provide dynamic web page functionality using the new HTML5 APIs.

- HyperText Transfer Protocol (HTTP) is the common communication standard used by web servers.

- Uniform Resource Locator (URL) is an absolute web address comprising protocol, domain, and path components.

- A relative address can reference an adjacent file by its file name and may use the syntax "../" to reference a parent directory.

- Web servers send response headers back to the requesting computer and a copy of the file requested, or an error code.

- Each HTML5 document should have a document type declaration, head section, and body section.

- Information about the document itself is contained within the head section, and content is contained within the body section.

- The document's written language is specified to the **lang** attribute in the opening **<html>** root element tag.

- The document's character-set encoding is specified to the **charset** attribute in a **<meta>** tag, within the head section.

- The document's title is specified between **<title>** **</title>** tags, within the head section.

- The free online W3C validator tool should be used to verify that the HTML5 document is free of errors.

- HTML5 documents can be created in a plain text editor or a specialized HTML editor such as Microsoft Expression Web.

2 Providing page information

This chapter demonstrates how the head section of an HTML5 document can describe the document, incorporate scripts for functionality, and add style sheets for presentation.

24   Bestowing a title

26   Specifying a character set

28   Refreshing the page

30   Describing the document

32   Incorporating scripts

34   Incorporating style sheets

36   Linking more resources

38   Summary

Bestowing a title

You can find a chart of all character entities at dev.w3.org/html5/html-author/charref

Don't forget

The specifications do not define a naming scheme for document titles, but do encourage authors to consider accessibility issues in all aspects of their web page designs.

The specifications require every HTML5 document to have a title, but its importance is often overlooked. The document title should be carefully considered, however, as it is used extensively:

● **Bookmarks** – save the document title to link back to its URL

● **Title Bar** – a web browser window may display the title

● **Navigation Tab** – a web browser tab may display the title

● **History** – saves the document title to link back to its URL

● **Search Engines** – read the document title and typically display it in search results to link back to its URL

Document titles should ideally be short and meaningful – each tab on a modern tabbed browser may display only 10 characters.

Document titles throughout a website should follow a consistent naming convention and capitalize all major words. One popular naming convention provides a personal or company name and brief page description separated by a hyphen. For example, "Amazon - HTML5 in easy steps". An alternative places the description first, so it remains visible when the title is truncated. For example, "HTML5 in easy steps - Amazon".

Hot tip

Title text that is not visible on the tab will still be read by a narrator. Press **WinKey** + **Enter** to launch the narrator on Windows 10, then click the tab to hear the title.

Document titles, and document content, may contain special characters that are known in HTML5 as "entities". Each entity reference begins with an ampersand and ends with a semi-colon. For example, the entity < (less than) creates a "<" character and the entity > (greater than) creates a ">" character. These are often needed to avoid confusion with the angled brackets that surround each HTML tag. Other frequently used entities include   (a single non-breaking space), © (©), ® (®), and ™ (™). These are best avoided in document titles, however, as the vocal narrator used by visually impaired viewers may read each entity character as a word.

1 Start a new HTML5 with a document type declaration
<!DOCTYPE HTML>

title.html

2 Add a root element containing head and body sections
<html lang="en">

<head>
<!-- Data describing the document to be added here -->
</head>

<body>
<!-- Content to appear in the browser to be added here -->
</body>

</html>

3 Within the head section, insert a meta element specifying the character set and an empty title element
<meta charset="UTF-8">
<title> </title>

The character set can be defined in uppercase, as shown here, or in lowercase as "utf-8".

4 Within the title element, insert a title including entities
<HTML5 in easy steps>

5 Save the document then open it in your web browser

`☐ <HTML5 in easy steps>  ✕  +`

6 Start a vocal narrator to hear that the title may be read out as "Less-than-HTML5-in-easy-steps-greater-than"

The vocal narrator on Windows 10 ignores angled brackets in a title, but they are read literally by the narrator in earlier versions of Windows.

7 Edit the document title to make it more user-friendly
"HTML5 in easy steps"

`☐ "HTML5 in easy steps"  ✕  +`

8 Save the document once more, then open it in your web browser to hear the narrator now read the document title as "HTML5 in easy steps"

25

Specifying a character set

The examples in this book are each files saved with Unicode endings using the UTF-8 character-set. This character-set supports all characters in both Western and English languages, which allows the HTML document to contain characters from any language. Further character sets exist that also support all languages, while others exclusively support Western languages. The five most popular character-sets are listed below:

Name:	Character Set:
UTF-8	Multi-lingual Universal Transformation Format
BIG5	Multi-lingual traditional Chinese characters
SHIFT_JIS	Multi-lingual traditional Japanese characters
US-ASCII	US ASCII standard Western alphabet characters
ISO-8859-1	ISO standard Western alphabet characters

Character-set names are not case-sensitive – so "BIG5", "Big5", and "big5" are equivalent.

Although UTF-8 supports Chinese and Japanese characters, they may appear as a simplified equivalent of those in the more specialized character sets, which create traditional characters.

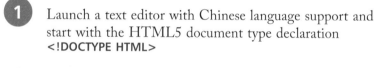

big5.html

1. Launch a text editor with Chinese language support and start with the HTML5 document type declaration
`<!DOCTYPE HTML>`

2. Add a root element containing head and body sections
`<html lang="en">`
`<head> <!-- Information goes here --> </head>`
`<body> <!-- Content goes here --> </body>`
`</html>`

3. Within the head section, insert a meta element to specify the character set as BIG5, and add a document title
`<meta charset="BIG5">`
`<title>BIG5 Encoding</title>`

4. In the body section, insert an English heading and its Chinese equivalent
`<h1>Fantastic Web Page</h1>`
`<h1> 神乎其神 網頁 </h1>`

5 Now, save the document as "big5.html" – being sure to set the encoding to BIG5

6 Next, recreate the HTML5 document, but this time specify the character set as UTF-8

utf-8.html

```
<!DOCTYPE HTML>
<html lang="en">
<head>
  <meta charset="UTF-8">
  <title>UTF-8 Encoding</title>
</head>
<body>
  <h1>Fantastic Web Page</h1>
  <h1> 神乎其神 網頁 </h1>
</body>
</html>
```

7 Save the second document as "utf-8.html" – being sure to set the encoding to UTF-8

8 Finally, open both documents in your web browser and compare the appearance of the characters created by the two different character-set encodings

US ASCII was formerly the most commonly used encoding on the web, but it has now been surpassed by UTF-8 due to its wider support.

Refreshing the page

Meta information is simply data that describes other data. In the context of HTML, document meta data describes the document itself – rather than the document's contents.

HTML meta data is defined in the head section of the HTML document using the **<meta>** tag. Previous examples have used this tag to specify the document's character-set – as one piece of information describing that document. Further **<meta>** tags can be added to describe other aspects of the document.

The **<meta>** tag is an "empty" tag that needs no matching closing tag to create an HTML element. It is only used to specify information with its tag attributes. For example, its **http-equiv** attribute can represent a document HTTP header property and its **content** attribute specify that property's value.

Assigning the HTTP "refresh" property to a **<meta>** tag's **http-equiv** attribute can be used to reload the page after a number of seconds specified by its **content** attribute. For example, to reload the page after five seconds, like this:

```
<meta http-equiv="refresh" content= "5">
```

This technique is often used on websites to dynamically update news or status items, as it does not depend on JavaScript support. Another popular use redirects the browser to a new web page after a specified number of seconds, like this:

```
<meta http-equiv="refresh" content= "5 ; url='new-page.html' ">
```

In this case, the **<meta>** tag's **content** attribute specifies both the number of seconds to delay and the new URL to load.

The W3C discourages the use of meta refresh as it can disorient users – but the meta refresh uses described here are considered legitimate.

refresh.html

1 Start with the HTML5 document type declaration
```
<!DOCTYPE HTML>
```

2 Add a root element containing head and body sections
```
<html lang="en">
<head>
<title>Refresh Example</title>
</head>
<body>
<h1>Moving in 5 Seconds...</h1>
</body>
</html>
```

...cont'd

3 Within the head section, insert meta elements to specify the encoding character set and refresh information
```
<meta charset="UTF-8">

<meta http-equiv="refresh"
        content="5 ; url='new-page.html' ">
```

4 Save the document as "refresh.html", then create the HTML document to which the browser will redirect
```
<!DOCTYPE HTML>
<html lang="en">
<head>
<meta charset="UTF-8">
<title>Refresh Example - New</title>
</head>
<body>
<h1>Moved Here After 5 Seconds!</h1>
</body>
</html>
```

new-page.html

5 Save the second document as "new-page.html", in the same directory as "refresh.html", then open the first document in your browser to see the browser get redirected after a five second delay

Notice that the **content** attribute value entirely surrounds both the delay and URL with double quote marks, but the URL is just surrounded by single quote marks.

Describing the document

In addition to specifying the document's character-set and expiry date, **<meta>** tags can be used to provide descriptive information that may be useful to search engines. This offers no guarantee of high ranking, however, as search engines also use other page information for that purpose – especially the document title. Nevertheless, it is helpful to provide a description and a list of keywords relevant to the contents of that page so that search engine "spiders" might usefully add the page to their index.

Descriptive **<meta>** tags always have a **name** attribute, to specify a page feature, and a **content** attribute to specify that feature's value. For example, the "description" name allows you to specify text content describing the page. This should be short, succinct sentences that might appear in a search engine's results page. Any description longer than around 200 characters may get truncated.

Similarly, the "keywords" name allows you to specify text content in the format of a comma-separated list of relevant keywords. These may be used by search engines to influence their results. For example, a search for "italian ceramics" could return all web pages with "italian" and "ceramics" in their keywords list. Promotion of the web page by keywords is best achieved by following some simple guidelines:

● Use only lowercase characters

● Keep all keywords on a single line

● Never repeat a keyword in a list

● Limit the keywords list to 1,000 characters or less

● Try to use the plural form for keywords – to match searches made with both the single and plural forms of that word

To specify that a web page should not be indexed by search engines, the "robots" name should have a content value of "noindex". Conversely, this may be set to "all" to explicitly allow indexing, but as that is the default state it's not really necessary.

1 Start with the HTML5 document type declaration
```
<!DOCTYPE HTML>
```

keywords.html

2 Add a root element containing head and body sections
```
<html lang="en">
<head>
  <title>Tuscan Home Decor [Italian Ceramics]</title>
</head>
<body> <h1>Beautiful Tuscan Ceramics</h1> </body>
</html>
```

Notice that the first four meta keywords in this example also appear in the meta description.

3 Within the head section, insert meta elements to specify the encoding character-set, description, and keywords
```
<meta charset="UTF-8">

<meta name="description"
content="Shop for beautiful Italian Ceramics,
          Tuscan Majolica, Home Decor, and more.">

<meta name="keywords"
content="tuscan,italian,ceramics,home decor,majolica,
          dinnerwares,vases,plates,bowls">
```

4 Save the document, then open it with Firefox and use the Page Info dialog on the context menu to see the meta data

There are a number of free meta tag generators available online – enter "free meta tag generator" into a search engine.

Incorporating scripts

Scripts can be incorporated within HTML documents to interact with the user and to provide dynamic effects. This ability has become increasingly important with the development of Web 2.0 pages in which sections of the page can be dynamically updated. Previously, the browser would typically request an entire new page from the web server, which was less efficient and more cumbersome, so Web 2.0 is a great improvement.

Scripts enclosed by **<script> </script>** tags can be added within the head section of an HTML document but, in line with the aim of HTML5 to separate content from presentation, are best contained in a separate file. The **<script>** tag automatically assumes a **type** attribute value of **"text/javascript"**, as scripts are expected to use the JavaScript language by default. This means that the **type** attribute can be omitted from the tag unless you are incorporating a script that uses a different scripting language. The URL of the script file must be assigned to a **src** attribute within the **<script>** tag when incorporating an external script. For example, add an adjacent script file named "script.js", like this:

```
<script src="script.js"></script>
```

Alternative fallback content can be provided in the document's body section between **<noscript></noscript>** tags, which will only be displayed when script functionality is absent or disabled.

script.html

1 Start with the HTML5 document type declaration
```
<!DOCTYPE HTML>
```

2 Add a root element containing head and body sections
```
<html lang="en">
<head>
  <meta charset="UTF-8">
  <title>JavaScript Example</title>
</head>
<body>
  <h1>Static</h1> <h1>Dynamic</h1>
</body>
</html>
```

3 In the head section, insert an element to incorporate an external JavaScript file
```
<script src="script.js"> </script>
```

4 In the body section, insert a fallback message
`<noscript>JavaScript Is Not Enabled!</noscript>`

5 Save the HTML5 document then open a new text editor
window and copy this script, exactly as it is listed

script.js

```
function init()
{
  var h1tags = document.getElementsByTagName("h1") ;
  h1tags[1].onclick = react ;
}

function react()
{
  this.innerHTML = "Clicked!" ; this.style.color = "red" ;
}
onload = init ;
```

6 Save the JavaScript file as "script.js" in the same directory
as the HTML5 document, then open the web page in
your browser and click on the second heading

Hot tip

You can learn more
about scripting with the
companion book in this
series JavaScript in easy
steps.

This script attaches a behavior to the second heading element, so
when it gets clicked by the user its text content and color change.

Incorporating style sheets

Style sheets can be incorporated within HTML documents to control the presentational aspects of each element on the page. The use of style sheets has replaced all features of HTML that formerly related to presentation. For example, the **<font>** tag has become obsolete, as font family, weight, style, and size are now specified by a style sheet rule.

Style sheets enclosed by **<style>** **</style>** tags can be added within the head section of an HTML document to enclose rules governing how the content will appear. The **<style>** tag automatically assumes a **type** attribute value of **"text/css"**, as style sheets are expected to use the Cascading Style Sheet language by default. This means that the **type** attribute can be omitted from the tag unless you are incorporating a style sheet that uses a different styling language. For example, a simple style sheet containing rules to determine the appearance of all size-one headings could look like this:

<style>

h1 { color : red ; background : yellow ; }

</style>

This is acceptable and will validate but, in line with the aim of HTML5 to separate content from presentation, style sheets are best contained within a separate file. The great advantage of placing style sheets and scripts in separate files is that they can be applied to multiple HTML documents – thus making website maintenance much easier. Editing a shared style sheet or script instantly affects each HTML document that shares that file.

Hot tip

The **<link>** tag is a single tag – it does not have a matching closing tag. See the element tags list on the inside front cover of this book to find other single tags.

An external style sheet is incorporated within an HTML document by adding a **<link>** tag in the document's head section. This must contain a **rel** (relationship) attribute assigned a **"stylesheet"** value, and the URL of the style sheet must be assigned to its **href** attribute. Once again, this tag automatically assumes a **type** attribute value of **"text/css"** for style sheets, so the **type** attribute can be omitted unless you are incorporating a style sheet that uses a different styling language. For example, add an adjacent style sheet file named "style.css", like this:

<link rel="stylesheet" href="style.css">

1 Start with the HTML5 document type declaration
`<!DOCTYPE HTML>`

style.html

2 Add a root element containing head and body sections
```
<html lang="en">
<head>
  <meta charset="UTF-8">
  <title>Style Sheet Example</title>
</head>
<body>
  <h1>Styled Heading</h1>
</body>
</html>
```

3 Within the head section, insert a link to an adjacent style sheet file
`<link rel="stylesheet" href="style.css">`

4 Save the HTML document, then open a new text editor window and precisely copy this style sheet
```
h1
{
        color : red ;
        background : yellow ;
        border : 10px dashed blue ;
        padding : 5px ;
        width : 550px ;
}
```

style.css

5 Save the Cascading Style Sheet file in the same directory as the HTML5 document, then open the web page in your browser to see the style rules applied

Coloring the **<h1>** element without setting a **width** rule would reveal that it occupies the entire width of the browser window – except for the default margins of the body.

Linking more resources

The **<link>** tag that was used in the previous example to incorporate a style sheet in an HTML5 document can also be used to incorporate other resources into a document.

This tag may only appear in the head section of a document, but the head section can contain many **<link>** tags. Each **<link>** tag must contain **rel** and **href** attributes, stating the relationship and location of the link resource, together with a **type** attribute where appropriate to specify the MIME type of the link resource.

Hot tip

MIME (Multipart Internet Mail Extension) types describe file types – such as **text/html** for HTML files. You can find the list of official MIME types at iana.org/assignments/media-types/media-types.xhtml

Permitted rel (relationship) values:				
alternate	author	bookmark	help	icon
license	next	nofollow	noreferrer	prev
search	stylesheet	tag		

Many of the link types above are intended to help search engines locate resources associated with that HTML document, and the **<link>** tag may also include a **title** attribute to further describe the resource. For example, a version of the page in another language:

```
<link rel="alternate" type="text/html" href="esp.html"
        title="Esta página en Español - This page in Spanish" >
```

The W3C HTML 5.1 specifications introduced a **rev** reverse link attribute for the **<link>** tag that can be used to specify how the document is related to the link.

In this case, the location of the resource is specified using a relative address that, by default, the browser will seek in the directory in which the HTML document is located. The browser can, however, be made to seek a relative address in a different directory by inserting a **<base>** tag at the start of the document's head section. Its **href** attribute can then specify the absolute directory address. For example, to specify a separate "resources" directory, like this:

```
<base href= "http://localhost/resources/">
```

Beware

When using a **<base>** element it must be placed in the head section before any **<link>** elements.

It is popular to link an icon resource to display in the web browser's address field. This can be placed in a directory specified by the **<base>** tag for most browsers, but Internet Explorer insists the icon is located in the web server's root directory and named exactly as "favicon.ico". All browsers do, however, recognize all other resources in the directory specified by the **<base>** tag.

...cont'd

1 Start with the HTML5 document type declaration
`<!DOCTYPE HTML>`

link.html

2 Add a root element containing head and body sections
```
<html lang="en">
<head>
  <meta charset="UTF-8">
  <title>Link Example</title>
</head>
<body>
  <h1>Linked Icon</h1>
</body>
</html>
```

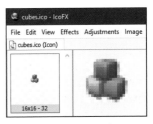

You can try IcoFX free for 30 days by download from **icofx.ro**

3 Within the head section, insert elements to specify a base "resources" directory and an icon resource
```
<base href="http://localhost/resources/">
<link rel="icon" href="cubes.ico">
```

4 Save the HTML document, then open an icon editor, such as IcoFX, and create an icon sized 16x16 pixels

5 Now, save the icon in the "resources" directory, named as "cubes.ico", and also save a copy in the root directory, named precisely as "favicon.ico" – for Internet Explorer

At the time of writing, this example is supported in all web browsers except Microsoft Edge.

6 Open the HTML document in your web browser via a web server to see the icon resource appear in the address field

This page is served to the browser by a local web server using the default "localhost" domain. Simply opening a local copy of this example in a browser will not display the icon.

37

Summary

- A document title is used by search engines and may be seen in a browser's title bar, navigation tab, bookmarks, and history.
- Document content and titles can include character entity references to display special characters, such as **©** for ©.
- Character-sets that support Eastern language characters often also support Western language characters.
- A **<meta>** tag can be used to refresh the page at a specified interval or to redirect the browser to a different page.
- Search engine spiders can use the keywords and description specified in **<meta>** tags to add a web page to their index.
- A keywords list should comprise only non-repeating lowercase keywords on a single line of the HTML document.
- Scripts can be added to the head section of an HTML5 document between **<script> </script>** tags, but are best created in a separate file for incorporation by this tag's **src** attribute.
- Style sheets can be added to the head section of an HTML5 document between **<style> </style>** tags, but are best created in a separate file for incorporation by a **<link>** tag.
- Editing a shared script or shared style sheet instantly affects each HTML document that shares that file – making website maintenance much easier.
- A **<link>** tag may only appear in the head section of an HTML document, and must contain **rel** and **href** attributes to describe the resource's relationship and location.
- A **<base>** tag can be added at the start of the head section to specify a particular directory in which to seek relative addresses.
- An icon link type can incorporate an icon named **favicon.ico** that may appear in the browser window and on favorite lists.

3 Creating body content

This chapter demonstrates how text and image elements can be created within the body section of an HTML5 document.

40 Working the body

42 Inserting paragraphs

44 Including quotations

46 Emphasizing text

48 Reading the small print

50 Marking text

52 Keeping preformatted text

54 Modifying text

56 Including code in text

58 Giving tooltip advice

60 Adding images

62 Directing languages

64 Summary

Working the body

Every HTML5 document should contain exactly one opening **<body>** tag and exactly one matching closing **</body>** tag – defining the body section to contain all document content that is intended for display in the web browser window.

The body section of an HTML document should not contain any meta data, scripts, or style sheets – **<meta>**, **<script>**, and **<link>** elements all belong in the head section.

Uniquely, the opening **<body>** tag may contain an attribute to reference the "load" event that occurs when the page has completely loaded in the web browser. The **onload** attribute is useful when scripting to respond to the load page event.

The **onload** attribute references the same load event that was used in the example on page 33 to create an "event-handler" function. Within the **<body>** tag, the **onload** attribute can specify the name of a script function to call when the load event occurs.

Alternatively, short script "snippets" can simply be assigned to the attributes within the HTML **<body>** tag. For example, the **onload** attribute could call upon the intrinsic **alert()** function to launch an alert dialog whenever that page gets loaded. This function can specify a message to be displayed by the dialog as a text string within quotes between the function parentheses.

With entire attribute values surrounded by double quotes, it is important to enclose the message text string within single quotes to avoid terminating the attribute value prematurely, like this:

<body onload= "alert('Greetings!')" >

If double quotes were used throughout in the example above, the attribute value would become **"alert("**. This principle of differentiating text strings must be applied to any attribute value that contains a "nested" quote.

The **onload** event call to the **alert()** function relies upon the browser being enabled for JavaScript in order to launch the dialog. A **<noscript>** element can be incorporated in the document body to advise the user when JavaScript is disabled.

Scripts and style sheets are best contained in separate files and incorporated into the HTML document by **<script>** and **<link>** elements placed within its head section.

In scripting terms, **onload** and **alert()** are both members of the **window** object, so you may find them written in scripts as **window.onload** and **window.alert()** – but as the **window** object is top-level in the document object hierarchy, the **window.** prefix is unnecessary.

The **onload** attribute is a remnant from earlier versions of HTML. It is better to specify event-handler functions in a script file – in line with the aim of HTML5 to separate content from presentation.

1 Start with the HTML5 document type declaration
```
<!DOCTYPE HTML>
```

body.html

2 Add a root element containing head and body sections
```
<html lang="en">
<head>
  <meta charset="UTF-8">
  <title>Body Attributes</title>
</head>
<body onload="alert( 'Greetings!' )" >
  <noscript>JavaScript Is Not Enabled!</noscript>
  <h1>Page Loaded</h1>
</body>
</html>
```

3 Save the HTML document, then open it in your web browser to see the alert dialog appear when it loads

Beware

The alert dialog is "modal" – the user must click OK to close it before the page will completely load.

4 Close the alert dialog, then disable JavaScript support and reload the page to see the advisory message

Hot tip

With the Firefox web browser, shown here, enter **about:config** in its address bar, then accept the "risk" warning and click the **javascript:enabled** item to **false** – to disable JavaScript support.

Inserting paragraphs

All text content is traditionally separated into sentences and paragraphs, to be more easily read and more readily understood. This is also true for text content in HTML5 documents, and their paragraphs are contained within **<p> </p>** tags. Each paragraph element is visually separated from the next one by the browser – typically leaving two empty lines between them.

Text within a paragraph will normally automatically wrap to the next line when it meets the element's edge, but it can be forced to wrap sooner by inserting a line break **
** tag.

For emphasis, a horizontal rule **<hr>** tag can be inserted between paragraphs to draw a line separating them. The **<hr>** tag cannot, however, be inserted inside a paragraph to separate sentences. You may be surprised to find the **<hr>** tag in HTML5, as it would seem to perform a purely presentational function. It is, however, described in the specifications as representing a "paragraph-level thematic break", such as a scene change in a story.

The **
** tag and **<hr>** tag are both single tags that need no matching closing tag.

para.html

1 Start with the HTML5 document type declaration
<!DOCTYPE HTML>

2 Add a root element containing head and body sections
```
<html lang="en">
<head>
  <meta charset="UTF-8">
  <title>Paragraph Example</title>
</head>
<body>
  <!-- Heading and paragraphs to be inserted here -->
</body>
</html>
```

3 Insert a large heading within the body section
<h1>The Statue of Liberty</h1>

4 Next, add a paragraph within the body section
<p>The Statue of Liberty was built over nine years by French sculptor Auguste Bartholdi. Upon its completion in 1884 all 350 individual pieces of the statue were packed into 214 crates for the long boat ride from France to New York.</p>

5 After the paragraph, add a horizontal ruled line
`<hr>`

6 After the horizontal ruled line, add a second paragraph
`<p>The statue arrived in America several months later and was reconstructed on Liberty Island. Auguste Bartholdi thought that the New York harbor was the perfect setting for his masterpiece because it was where immigrants got their first view of the New World.</p>`

7 Now, insert breaks into the paragraphs to control the length of their lines
`<p>The Statue of Liberty was built over nine years by French sculptor Auguste Bartholdi.<br>Upon its completion in 1884 all 350 individual pieces of the statue were packed into <br>214 crates for the long boat ride from France to New York.</p>`

`<p>The statue arrived in America several months later and was reconstructed on <br>Liberty Island. Auguste Bartholdi thought that the New York harbor was the perfect <br>setting for his masterpiece because it was where immigrants got their first view of <br>the New World.</p>`

8 Save the HTML document, then open it in your web browser to see the heading, paragraphs, forced line breaks, and horizontal ruled line

The **`<hr>`** element can be considered to be the HTML equivalent of the *** section separator often found in stories and essays.

43

Including quotations

It is important to recognize that some HTML5 elements produce a rectangular block area on the page in which to display content, while others merely produce a small block on a line within an outer containing block. These are referred to as "flow" and "phrasing" elements. Phrasing elements, which produce a small block on a line, must always be enclosed by a flow element, which produces the larger containing block, such as **<p> </p>**. The difference between flow elements and phrasing elements can be seen by contrasting how web browsers display the two HTML elements that are used to include quotations in documents.

The **<blockquote> </blockquote>** tags are intended to surround long quotations from another source, which can be specified by its **cite** attribute. For this element, the browser typically produces a rectangular block area to contain the quotation, starting on a new line and indented from surrounding content – so **<blockquote>** is a flow element.

The **<q> </q>** tags, on the other hand, are intended to surround short quotations from another source, which can be specified by its **cite** attribute. For this element, the browser typically produces a small block area on the current line to contain the quotation – so **<q>** is a phrasing element.

Unlike the **<blockquote>** flow element, the **<q>** phrasing element causes the browser to automatically add quotation marks around the element's content when it gets displayed on the page. Ideally, these should be double quotation marks surrounding the entire element content, and single quotation marks around any inner nested quotations, but its implementation may vary.

quote.html

1 Start with the HTML5 document type declaration
<!DOCTYPE HTML>

2 Add a root element containing head and body sections
```
<html lang="en">
<head>
 <meta charset="UTF-8">
 <title>Quotation Example</title>
</head>
<body>
 <p>A Paragraph Flow Block!</p>
</body>
</html>
```

3 Within the body section insert a blockquote containing two small nested quotations
```
<blockquote cite="http://www.example.com/origin.html">
A Blockquote Flow Block!<br>Paul said, <q>I saw Emma
at lunch, she told me <q>Susan wants you to get some
ice cream on your way home.</q> I think I will get some
at Ben and Jerry's on Main Street.</q> </blockquote>
```

4 Save the HTML document, then open it to compare the double quote marks, single quote marks, and apostrophe

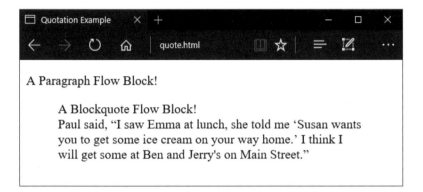

5 Insert this style sheet into the head section of the document, then reload the page to reveal the blocks
```
<style>
p, blockquote { border: 1px solid red ; }
q { background : aqua; }
</style>
```

By default, the paragraph element block will fill the width of its containing element – like the **<h1>** element block in the example on page 35.

The flow elements are shown here with red solid borders, and the phrasing elements with a light blue background.

Emphasizing text

HTML5 provides four phrasing elements that can be used to emphasize text within the body of a document:

● Text enclosed between **\<b> \</b>** tags is enhanced without conveying extra importance, such as keywords in a paragraph – typically displayed in a bold font.

● Text enclosed between **\<i> \</i>** tags is enhanced without conveying extra importance, such as technical terms in a paragraph – typically displayed in an italic font.

● Text enclosed between **\<strong> \</strong>** tags gains increased importance, without changing the meaning of the sentence – typically displayed in a bold font.

● Text enclosed between **\<em> \</em>** tags should be stressed to deliberately affect the meaning of the sentence – typically displayed in an italic font.

It is perhaps surprising that the **\<b>** and **\<i>** tags remain in HTML5, as they outwardly suggest that content should be presented in a bold or italic font – contradicting the aim of HTML5 to separate structure from presentation. According to the specifications, their meaning has been redefined, however, so content within a **\<b>** element should be "stylistically offset" and that within an **\<i>** element should be seen as in an "alternate voice". In real terms, these are nonetheless represented by bold and italic fonts but should only be used as a last resort as they do not convey meaning – use **\<strong>** and **\<em>** tags instead.

The advantage of the **\<strong>** and **\<em>** tags is that they describe the importance of their content relative to surrounding text, and let the browser choose how it should be presented. Additionally, these tags are more relevant to suggest how narrators should convey their content vocally.

As with many HTML tags, the **\<strong>** and **\<em>** tags can be nested, but care must be taken to close nested elements correctly. For example, **\<strong>\<em>...\</em>\</strong>** is the correct order, whereas **\<strong>\<em>...\</strong>\</em>** is incorrect and will not validate.

Don't forget

The specifications encourage web page authors to consider accessibility issues in all aspects of their web page designs.

1 Start with the HTML5 document type declaration
```
<!DOCTYPE HTML>
```

emphasis.html

2 Add a root element containing head and body sections
```
<html lang="en">
<head>
  <meta charset="UTF-8">
  <title>Emphasis Example</title>
</head>
<body>
 <!-- Document content to be added here -->
</body>
</html>
```

3 Within the body section, add a paragraph that emphasizes some text without affecting the meaning of the sentence
```
<p><strong>Warning.</strong> This dungeon is
dangerous.<strong>Avoid the ducks.</strong> Take any
gold you find.<strong>Do not take any of the diamonds,
they are explosive.</strong> You have been warned.</p>
```

4 Next, within the body section, add paragraphs that emphasize some text to affect the meaning of the sentence
```
<p><em>Puppy dogs</em> are cute.</p>
<p>Puppy dogs <em>are</em> cute.</p>
<p>Puppy dogs are <em>cute.</em></p>
```

The **<b>** tag should be avoided wherever possible, but one legitimate use is to markup the lead sentence of an article.

5 Save the HTML document, then open it in your web browser to see how the text has been emphasized

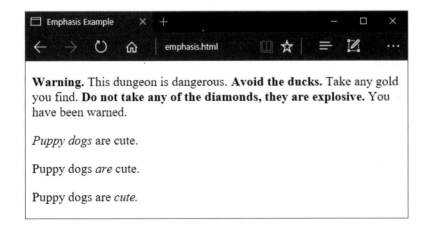

47

Reading the small print

HTML5 provides three elements that can be used to format text within the body of a document:

- Text enclosed between **<small> </small>** tags is regarded as a side comment to surrounding text, such as copyright information – typically displayed in a smaller font.

- Text enclosed within **<del> </del>** tags is regarded as having been removed from the document, such as a completed item in a to-do list – typically displayed with a strike-through line.

- Text enclosed within **<ins> </ins>** tags is regarded as having been added to the document, such as a new additional item in a "to do" list – typically displayed with an underline.

The **<small>** tag is only meant to contain short comments that supplement surrounding content. It is not intended for use with large sections of text, such as multiple paragraphs, as that would be considerably more than a side comment.

In displaying content contained within a **<small>** element, the web browser considers the size of the font used to display the surrounding content, then applies an appropriate reduction. Therefore, where the surrounding content is displayed with a font of 12-point size, content contained within a **<small>** element might be displayed with a font of 10-point size – the precise size is determined by the browser.

Both **<del>** and **<ins>** elements can be used within a section of content, to mark up snippets of changed text, and to enclose entire sections of changed content, such as replaced paragraphs.

The **<del>** and **<ins>** tags may optionally include a **cite** attribute to specify the URL of a document explaining the changes made.

48

format.html

1 Start with the HTML5 document type declaration
<!DOCTYPE HTML>

2 Add a root element containing head and body sections
<html lang="en">
<head>
  <meta charset="UTF-8"><title>Format Example</title>
</head>
<body> <!-- Content to be added here --> **</body>**
</html>

3 Within the body section, insert a paragraph containing a side comment for legal purposes
```
<p>Example Corp today announced record profits for
the second quarter <small>(Full Disclosure: EG News
is a subsidiary of Example Corp)</small>, leading to
speculation about a merger with Demo Group.</p>
```

4 Next, insert a large heading and a regular paragraph
```
<h1>To Do List</h1>
<p>Empty the dishwasher</p>
```

5 Now, insert a paragraph that has been deleted
```
<del><p>Take out the trash</p></del>
```

6 Then, insert a paragraph that has been added
```
<ins><p>Sweep the yard</p></ins>
```

7 Finally, insert a paragraph that has been added, which contains a text snippet that has been changed
```
<ins>
<p>Feed the <del>dog</del><ins> cat</ins></p>
</ins>
```

8 Save the HTML document, then open it in your web browser to see how the text has been formatted

The **<big>** and **<tt>** tags in the previous version of HTML are now obsolete, as they were seen as presentational.

The **<small>** tag does not denote content of lesser importance, only that it is a side comment to surrounding text.

Marking text

HTML5 provides four phrasing elements that can be used to mark text for special treatment within the body of a document:

- Text enclosed between **<s> </s>** tags is marked as being superseded by more accurate or relevant up-to-date content – typically displayed with a strike-through line.

- Text enclosed between **<u> </u>** tags is marked as being different in some way to normal text content – typically displayed with an underscore line to underline the text.

- Text enclosed between **<mark> </mark>** is marked as being of special significance for reference – typically displayed in a colored background block to highlight the text.

- Text broken by a **<wbr>** tag is invisibly marked as being a suitable point at which to break a line of text – representing a word-break opportunity.

It is important to note that specifications state that the **<s>** tag should not be used to indicate edited content within a document. The **<del>** tag should be used instead to indicate document edits.

Similarly, the **<mark>** tag should not be used to emphasize the importance of text content, but should only be used to highlight the relevance of text within a document. The **<strong>** and **<em>** tags should be used instead to indicate emphasis.

The **<u>** tag was deprecated in the HTML 5.0 specification, as underlined text within a document traditionally indicates hyperlinks. The **<u>** tag has, however, reappeared in the HTML 5.1 specification for the purposes of labeling misspelled words or proper names in Chinese. Authors are nonetheless strongly discouraged from using the **<u>** tag for emphasis, to avoid confusion with hyperlinks. Once again, the **<strong>** and **<em>** tags should be used instead to indicate emphasis.

Where the document contains lengthy content that may exceed the width of the browser, you may wish to use the **<wbr>** tag to indicate appropriate points at which a line-break can be inserted.

The **<s>**, **<mark>**, and **<wbr>** tags are new elements introduced in HTML 5.1, whereas the **<u>** tag has been reinstated in HTML 5.1 after previously being deprecated.

Use style sheet rules for presentation purposes rather than the **<u>** tag for underlines.

1 Start with the HTML5 document type declaration
```
<!DOCTYPE HTML>
```

mark.html

2 Add a root element containing head and body sections
```
<html lang="en">
<head>
  <meta charset="UTF-8">
  <title>Mark Example</title>
</head>
<body>
 <!-- Document content to be added here -->
</body>
</html>
```

3 Within the body section, add a paragraph that marks a word-break opportunity
```
<p>Microsoft Surface Pro 4
<wbr>- 128GB / Intel Core i5</p>
```

4 Next, within the body section, add a paragraph that marks a superseded price and provides a current price
```
<p><s>$999</s> $799</p>
```

5 Now, within the body section, add paragraphs that mark text for reference and mark a misspelled word
```
<p>Memory: <mark>4GB</mark>
<br>Screen: <mark>12.3-inch</mark></p>
<p>Surface <u>Penn</u> Included</p>
```

6 Save the HTML document then open it in your web browser to see how the text has been marked

Suggesting word-break opportunities with **<wbr>** is particularly suitable for small devices, but implementation is dependent upon support for this feature in the browser.

51

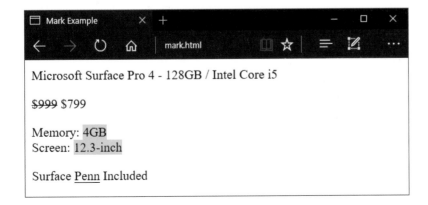

Keeping preformatted text

Where it is desirable to have the browser render text content that has been "preformatted", the web page author can enclose that content between **<pre> </pre>** flow element tags. These advise the browser that the following instructions should be applied:

- Preserve white space

- Render all text with a fixed-width font

- Disable automatic word-wrapping

- Do not disable bi-directional processing

Preserving the white space retains all spaces, tabs and line breaks. This is great to display lengthy poems in which every second line is indented. For example, with this verse:

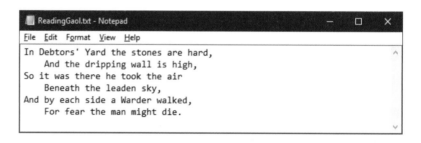

In this case, each second line is indented by four character widths – created by hitting the space bar four times to insert four invisible space characters. These indents will be exactly preserved by the **<pre>** element as four character widths.

Tab characters, on the other hand, can present some surprises as they are usually interpreted by a browser as eight character widths. This agrees with the tab size in Windows' Notepad application but other text editors can vary. This means that preformatted text containing tab characters may appear to be mis-aligned by the **<pre>** element. It is for this reason that the specifications discourage the use of tab characters when creating preformatted text content.

The **<pre> </pre>** tags can also be useful to ensure "Text-Art", sometimes used as web forum signatures, will appear as intended.

Use spaces rather than tabs when preparing preformatted text.

1 Start with the HTML5 document type declaration
```
<!DOCTYPE HTML>
```

preformat.html

2 Add a root element containing head and body sections
```
<html lang="en">
<head>
  <meta charset="UTF-8">
  <title>Preformat Example</title>
</head>
<body> <!-- Content to be added here --> </body>
</html>
```

3 Within the body section, insert a document heading
```
<h1>Text-Art Signature</h1>
```

4 Ensure that the font in your text editor is set to a fixed width font, such as Lucida Console for Notepad

Notice that **<pre>** is a flow element so it does not need to be enclosed within a paragraph – it creates its own block.

5 Next, in the body section, insert a **<pre>** element containing preformatted content in a fixed width font – and produced without any tab characters

```
<pre>
</pre>
```

53

6 Save the HTML document, then open it in your web browser to ensure the content retains preformatting

You can use any character within a fixed width font to create your Text-Art – Windows users can use the Character Map program in System Tools to select special characters from the Lucida Console font.

Modifying text

Regular text in a paragraph area of a web page is displayed in invisible inline phrasing boxes that comprise an outer logical box, and an inner font box containing a baseline:

An inline phrasing box.

Logical box
Baseline
Font box

The vertical line spacing is determined by the font height to allow space between characters that extend below the baseline, such as "p", and tall characters that extend upwards, such as "b", plus a vertical margin area.

> Text in a paragraph written in an inline phrasing box.
> Lines are spaced so characters do not collide. ™

Additionally, the font box will accommodate "superscript", such as the trade mark symbol ™ produced by the **™** character entity. Superscript is any text, number or symbol that appears smaller than regular text and is set above the baseline. Mathematical formulae can use superscript to indicate numeric powers with the character entities **²** for ^{2} and **³** for ^{3}. The font box will also accommodate "subscript" – that appears smaller than regular text and is set below the baseline.

The height available for superscript and subscript with the standard vertical line spacing is limited so the character size is restricted. Rather than use character entities for this purpose, it is often better to use the HTML5 **** tags for superscript and **** tags for subscript. These elements increase the vertical line spacing to allow more prominent superscript and subscript characters. For example, **²** is larger than **²**. Additionally, any content can be included within these elements so you are not restricted to available character entity references.

> Lines are spaced so characters do not collide with the superscript below.
> Text line in a paragraph containing ^{superscript} and $_{\text{subscript}}$
> Lines are spaced so characters do not collide with the subscript above.

1 Start with the HTML5 document type declaration
```
<!DOCTYPE HTML>
```

modify.html

2 Add a root element containing head and body sections
```
<html lang="en">
<head>
  <meta charset="UTF-8">
  <title>Modify Text Example</title>
</head>
<body> <!-- Content to be added here --> </body>
</html>
```

3 Within the body section, insert a paragraph containing superscript produced by character entities
```
<p>Square of four: 4&sup2; = 16 <br>
        Cube of four: 4&sup3; = 64</p>
```

4 Now, in the body section, insert a similar paragraph containing superscript produced by HTML elements
```
<p>Square of four: 4<sup>2</sup> = 16 <br>
        Cube of four: 4<sup>3</sup> = 64</p>
```

5 Finally, in the body section, insert a paragraph containing subscript produced by HTML elements
```
<p>Water: H<sub>2</sub>O <br>
        Oil of Vitriol: H<sub>2</sub>SO<sub>4</sub>
</p>
```

6 Save the document, then open it in your browser to compare the superscript and to see the subscript text

Hot tip

When using superscript ^{2} in paragraphs to denote area, such as 10 feet^2, you may prefer to use the entity **²** rather than **²** to keep line spacings equal.

55

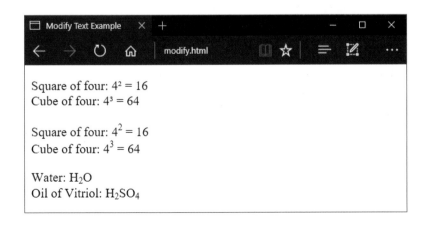

Modify Text Example   modify.html

Square of four: $4^2 = 16$
Cube of four: $4^3 = 64$

Square of four: $4^2 = 16$
Cube of four: $4^3 = 64$

Water: H_2O
Oil of Vitriol: H_2SO_4

Hot tip

The datetime value of a **<time>** element must be in a valid format, for example, as full datetime with **2017-12-25 14:30** or month as **2017-12** or date as **2017-12-25** or day with **12-25** or time only as **14:30**.

Including code in text

HTML5 provides five phrasing elements specifically to include computer program code within the body of a document:

- Complete program code, or snippets, can be enclosed between **<code> </code>** tags for displaying in a suitable font.

- Program variable instances can be enclosed between **<var> </var>** tags to differentiate them from regular text.

- Sample program input and output can be enclosed between **<samp> </samp>** tags to differentiate them from regular text.

- Content that also has associated machine-readable code can be enclosed between **<data> </data>** tags and the code specified to its required **value** attribute.

- Dates and times can be enclosed in **<time> </time>** tags and a machine-readable version specified to its **datetime** attribute.

The **<data>** element could, for example, describe a book title and its machine-readable ISBN, then the **<time>** element could describe that book's publication date:

code.html

1 Start with the HTML5 document type declaration
<!DOCTYPE HTML>

2 Add a root element containing head and body sections
```
<html lang="en">
<head>
  <meta charset="UTF-8">
  <title>Program Code Example</title>
</head>
<body> <!-- Content to be added here --> </body>
</html>
```

3 In the body section, insert a program description containing variables, sample input, and sample output
```
<p>
This program assigns an input value to <var>degF</var>
then performs a conversion on that value, assigning the
result to <var>degC</var> for output.
For example, input of <samp>98.6</samp>
will output <samp>37C</samp>.
</p>
```

4 Next, in the body section, insert preformatted program code

```
<pre>
<code>
#include &lt;iostream&gt;
using namespace std;

int main()
{
  float degF, degC;
  cout &lt;&lt; "Enter Fahrenheit Temperature: ";
  cin &gt;&gt; degF;
  degC = ((degF - 32.0 ) * (5.0 / 9.0));
  cout &lt;&lt; degF &lt;&lt; "F is " &lt;&lt; degC &lt;&lt; "C";
  cout &lt;&lt; endl;
  return 0;
}
</code>
</pre>
```

Note that all angled bracket characters in the program code have been replaced by character entities to avoid conflict with the HTML tags.

5 Now, in the body section, state the program code source

```
<data value="978-1-84078-719-1">
C++ Programming in easy steps, 5th Edition</data>
<time datetime="2016-12-15">
(December 15th, 2016)</time>
```

6 Save the HTML document, then open it in your web browser to see how the program description, code and source details appear

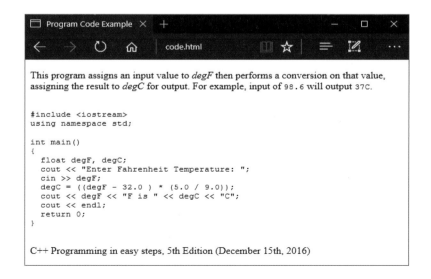

This program assigns an input value to *degF* then performs a conversion on that value, assigning the result to *degC* for output. For example, input of 98.6 will output 37C.

```
#include <iostream>
using namespace std;

int main()
{
  float degF, degC;
  cout << "Enter Fahrenheit Temperature: ";
  cin >> degF;
  degC = ((degF - 32.0 ) * (5.0 / 9.0));
  cout << degF << "F is " << degC << "C";
  cout << endl;
  return 0;
}
```

C++ Programming in easy steps, 5th Edition (December 15th, 2016)

Remember to insert the phrasing **<code>** element within a **<pre>** flow element to preserve the program code layout in an HTML document.

Giving tooltip advice

HTML5 provides four phrasing elements that can be used to designate advisory phrases within the body of a document:

- Text can be enclosed between **<abbr> </abbr>** tags to indicate it is an abbreviation.

- Text can be enclosed between **<cite> </cite>** tags to indicate it is a citation or reference from another source.

- Text can be enclosed between **<dfn> </dfn>** tags to indicate it is the definitive instance of that term.

- Text can be enclosed between **<kbd> </kbd>** tags to indicate input to be entered by the user from the keyboard.

Every HTML5 element that can legally appear within the body of a document may optionally include a **title** attribute. Values specified to a **title** attribute are typically displayed as a tooltip that pops up when the user places the cursor over the element. This means that each of the phrasing elements listed above can include a **title** attribute to expand on the meaning of its content.

advice.html

1 Start with the HTML5 document type declaration
<!DOCTYPE HTML>

2 Add a root element containing head and body sections
<html lang="en">
<head>
 <meta charset="UTF-8">
 <title>Advice Example</title>
</head>
<body> <!-- Content to be added here --> </body>
</html>

3 In the body section, insert a paragraph containing an abbreviation with tooltip advice
<p><abbr title="HyperText Markup Language">HTML
 </abbr>5 in easy steps</p>

4 Next, insert a citation reference with tooltip advice
<p><cite title="Inventor of the HyperText Markup Language">Sir Tim Berners-Lee</cite></p>

5 Now, insert a definitive term with tooltip advice
```
<p><dfn title="The popular language of the
WorldWideWeb. Commonly abbreviated to 'HTML'">
HyperText Markup Language</dfn></p>
```

6 Then, insert a keyboard instruction with tooltip advice
```
<p><kbd title="Press the Y key on your keyboard to
execute a script. This requires JavaScript to be enabled in
your browser">Hit Y to Continue.</kbd></p>
```

7 Finally, add an element in the head section to identify a
script that will respond to the keyboard instruction
```
<script src="advice.js"> </script>
```

8 Save the HTML document, then exactly copy the script
below and save it as "advice.js" alongside the HTML file
```
function showkey(e) {
var obj= ( navigator.appName ===
            "Microsoft Internet Explorer") ? event : e ;
if( obj.keyCode === 89 || obj.keyCode === 121 )
            alert( "Y pressed. Thank You." ) ;
}
document.onkeydown = showkey ;
```

9 Open the HTML document and place the cursor over
the elements to see the individual tooltips

10 With JavaScript support
enabled in your browser,
press the Y key to see
the script response

Remember to use single
quote marks for nested
quotes – as with 'HTML'
in Step 5.

advice.js

The script looks at the
keycode when the key
gets pressed and will
respond to lowercase "y"
and uppercase "Y".

Adding images

The ability to add images to HTML document content introduces lots of exciting possibilities. An image is easily added to the document using the **<img>** tag, which should preferably always include these attributes:

- An **src** attribute is required to specify the image location URL, by either its absolute or relative path.

- A **width** attribute is recommended to specify the pixel width of the area the image will occupy on the page.

- A **height** attribute is recommended to specify the pixel height of the area the image will occupy on the page.

- An **alt** attribute is recommended to specify text describing the image, for occasions when the image cannot be loaded.

The values assigned to the **width** and **height** attributes instruct the web browser to create a content area on the web page of that size. This need not be the actual dimensions of the image, as the web browser can render the image in another specified size. Care must be taken to avoid distortion by ensuring the dimensions are scaled in proportion to the actual image size. Additionally, images should only be scaled down, as scaling up often results in pixelation – where individual pixels are visible to the eye. It is inefficient, however, to rely upon the browser to scale images that are not to be displayed full size as this requires downloading unnecessarily larger files. It is better to adjust the image size to the actual dimensions it will occupy on the web page using a graphics editor, such as Photoshop, so it will download and display faster.

Attributes in HTML tags can appear in any order.

Avoid the BMP bitmap file format for web graphics – saving the original image shown here as **fish.bmp** creates a file size of 790KB!

Original file size	Item type: PNG File Dimensions: 600 x 449 Size: 124 KB
Reduced to 33%	Item type: PNG File Dimensions: 200 x 150 Size: 30.5 KB

The optimum file type for web bitmap graphics is the popular non-proprietary Portable Network Graphics (PNG) format, which produces compact files and supports transparency.

1 Start with the HTML5 document type declaration
`<!DOCTYPE HTML>`

image.html

2 Add a root element containing head and body sections
```
<html lang="en">
<head>
  <meta charset="UTF-8"> <title>Image Example</title>
</head>
<body> <!-- Content to be added here --> </body>
</html>
```

3 Within the body section, insert three image elements – to display a graphic at full size plus two scaled versions
```
<img src="fish.png" width="200" height="150" alt="Fish">
<img src="fish.png" width="150" height="112" alt="Fish">
<img src="fish.png" width="100" height="75"  alt="Fish">
```

4 Save the document, then open it in your browser to see the background shining through transparent image areas

Hot tip

To change Firefox's default background color, select the hamburger button, Options, Content, Colors, then click Background and choose a new color.

Directing languages

The recommended UTF-8 document encoding format provides support for bi-directional text, so that characters from languages written right-to-left, such as Hebrew, are automatically written in that direction and may appear alongside left-to-right text such as English. Content to be read in right-to-left direction should be enclosed within **<bdi> </bdi>** bi-directional isolation tags so as not to confuse the browser, as it expects to read left-to-right. Additionally, HTML5 provides a **<bdo>** bi-direction override element to which a text direction can be explicitly specified as either "ltr" or "rtl" by its **dir** attribute. The bi-direction override allows characters from right-to-left languages to be written as character entities in an HTML document in "logical" left-to-right order, but to be displayed in "visual" right-to-left order. For example, the **<bdo>** element below encloses five character entities from left-to-right, in the order they may have been entered, but displays them right-to-left:

<bdo dir="rtl">ישראל</bdo>

.... appears as ישראל (Yiśrāʼēl in the Latin alphabet).

Ruby annotation

For Eastern languages, HTML5 supports "ruby annotation" that usefully provides pronunciation alongside text. In Japanese, for example, there is more than one alphabet. Text written in the semantic "kanji" alphabet, which has thousands of characters, is often annotated with its equivalent in the phonetic "hiragana" language, which has around 50 characters, to aid pronunciation. This is called "furigana" in Japanese and "ruby" in English – named after the small font used to indicate the pronunciation. For the benefit of Westerners, the Japanese kanji text can be annotated with "romaji" – its Latin alphabet equivalent. Similarly in Chinese, text written in the "mandarin" alphabet can be annotated with "pinyin" – its Latin alphabet equivalent.

HTML5 ruby annotation is entirely enclosed between root **<ruby> </ruby>** tags. This element may then enclose the Eastern text within **<rb> </rb>** tags (ruby base) and the pronunciation between **<rt> </rt>** (ruby text) tags. Optionally, the entire **<rt>** element can be enclosed between **<rp> </rp>** (ruby parentheses) tags to display the pronunciation in parentheses after the main text in old browsers that do not support ruby annotation, and an English language equivalent provided within **<rtc> </rtc>** tags.

Without the bi-direction override, these character entities get displayed in their logical order as לארשי – which is back-to-front for the right-to-left Hebrew language.

Don't confuse ruby annotation with the unconnected Ruby programming language.

1 Start with the HTML5 document type declaration
<!DOCTYPE HTML>

ruby.html

2 Add a root element containing head and body sections
<html lang="en">
<head>
  <meta charset="UTF-8"> <title>Ruby Example</title>
</head>
<body> <!-- Content to be added here --> </body>
</html>

3 In the body section, insert an element for Japanese text
with its appropriate pronunciation annotation
<ruby> <rb>東京</rb> <rt>tō kyō</rt> </ruby>

4 Surround the pronunciation with ruby parentheses for
non-supporting browsers and add an English equivalent
<rp> (</rp> <rt>tō kyō</rt> <rp>)</rp>
<rtc>Tokyo</rtc>

5 Next, insert a complete ruby element for Chinese text
<ruby> <rb>北京</rb>
<rp> (</rp> <rt>běi jīng</rt> <rp>)</rp>
<rtc>Beijing</rtc> </ruby>

6 Save the document, then open it in different browsers to
compare how the ruby annotations get displayed

The ruby elements are
illustrated with an added
border style for clarity.

Summary

- The **<body>** element encloses all document content, and its opening tag may include an **onload** scripting attribute.

- A paragraph is enclosed within a **<p>** element and may use the **
** tag to force breaks between lines of text.

- Flow elements create a block area on the page, whereas phrasing elements create a small block on a line.

- Long quotations may be enclosed within a **<blockquote>** flow element, and short quotations within a **<q>** phrasing element.

- The **<em>** and **<strong>** phrasing elements are preferred over the **<i>** and **<b>** phrasing elements to emphasize text.

- Side comments can be enclosed within a **<small>** element and the **<ins>** and **<del>** elements used to indicate replaced text.

- The **<s>** element denotes superseded content, and the **<mark>** element is used to highlight content for reference.

- The **<wbr>** element can be used to suggest an appropriate point at which to break a word or line of text.

- To avoid mis-alignment, tab spacing should be avoided when creating preformatted text for inclusion within a **<pre>** element.

- Superscript and subscript can be included using character entities or using the **<sup>** and **<sub>** elements.

- Program code can be included in an HTML document using the **<code>**, **<var>** and **<samp>** elements.

- Machine-readable code can be specified to a **value** attribute of the **<data>** tag and to a **datetime** attribute of the **<time>** tag.

- The **<abbr>**, **<cite>**, **<dfn>** and **<kbd>** elements provide advice.

- Most elements that can appear in the document body can include a **title** attribute to provide tooltip text.

- The **<img>** tag places an image on the web page and should preferably always include **src, width, height** and **alt** attributes.

- The **<bdi>** and **<bdo>** bi-directionals element can be used to surround items of text written in a language read right-to-left.

- Ruby annotation uses **<ruby>**, **<rb>**, **<rt>**, **<rp>** and **<rtc>** elements to provide pronunciation aid for Eastern languages.

4 Inserting hyperlinks

This chapter demonstrates how to insert hyperlinks in an HTML5 document so the user can navigate around the web page or site.

66 Creating hyperlinks

68 Accessing links via keys

70 Linking to page fragments

72 Linking to protocols

74 Using images as hyperlinks

76 Producing image map links

78 Generating popups

80 Summary

Creating hyperlinks

When the internet carried only text content, "hypertext" provided the ability to easily access related documents and was fundamental to the creation of the World Wide Web. Today, images can also be used for this purpose, so any navigational element of a web page is now referred to as a "hyperlink".

Hyperlinks are enclosed between **<a> </a>** anchor tags, which specify the target URL to an **href** (hyperlink reference) attribute in the opening tag. The web browser will display a hyperlink in a manner that distinguishes it from regular text – typically hypertext gains an underline and image-based hyperlinks gain a colored border.

Each web page hyperlink is sensitive to three interactive states:

● **Hover** – gaining focus, the cursor is placed over the hyperlink.

● **Active** – retrieving the linked resource, the user clicks the hyperlink.

● **Visited** – the linked resource has previously been retrieved.

Style rules can be used to emphasize each hyperlink state:

hyperlink.html

1 Start with the HTML5 document type declaration
<!DOCTYPE HTML>

2 Add a root element containing head and body sections, with a link element pointing to a style sheet
```
<html lang="en">
<head>
<meta charset="UTF-8">
<title>Hyperlink Example</title>
<link rel="stylesheet" href="hyperlink.css">
</head>
<body>  <!-- Content to go here -->  </body>
</html>
```

3 Within the body section, insert a hyperlink to a target page, including tooltip advice
```
<a href="target.html"
title="A hyperlink to a target page">Visit Target</a>
```

...cont'd

4 Save the HTML document, then create a similar second document containing a link targeting the first document
```
<a href="hyperlink.html"
title="A hyperlink to return">Return</a>
```

target.html

5 Save the second HTML document, then create a style sheet to emphasize each hyperlink state
```
a:hover  { background : yellow ; }
a:active  { background : olive ;  }
a:visited { background : aqua ;   }
```

hyperlink.css

6 Save the style sheet, then open the first web page in your browser to see the hyperlink in its default state

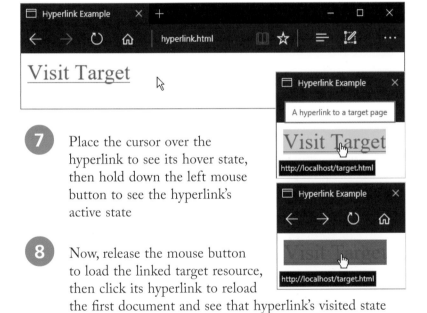

7 Place the cursor over the hyperlink to see its hover state, then hold down the left mouse button to see the hyperlink's active state

8 Now, release the mouse button to load the linked target resource, then click its hyperlink to reload the first document and see that hyperlink's visited state

The hyperlink on the target page instantly appears in the visited state because the browser recognizes that its return target has been previously visited.

Accessing links via keys

There are three ways to access the target of a hyperlink:

- **Pointer** – a mouse or similar device places a screen pointer over a hyperlink, then the user clicks to access its target.

- **Tab** – repeatedly hit the Tab key to successively focus on each hyperlink in turn, then hit Return to access the target of the currently selected hyperlink.

- **Access Key** – hit a designated character key to focus on a particular hyperlink, then hit Return to access its target.

A designated character key is specified for a hyperlink by the **accesskey** attribute of an **<a>** anchor tag. The method to utilize the designated key generally requires the user to press **ALT** + *accesskey* with most web browsers, such as Microsoft Edge and Google Chrome, but it's **ALT** + **SHIFT** + *accesskey* with Firefox.

access.html

1 Start with the HTML5 document type declaration
<!DOCTYPE HTML>

2 Add a root element containing head and body sections, with a link element pointing to a style sheet
```
<html lang="en">
<head>
<meta charset="UTF-8">
<title>Access Example</title>
<link rel="stylesheet" href="access.css">
</head>
<body>  <!-- Content to go here -->  </body>
</html>
```

3 Within the body section, insert two hyperlinks that designate different numeric access key characters
```
<a href="access.html" accesskey="1">Home Page</a> |
<a href="catalog.html" accesskey="2">Catalog Page</a>
```

catalog.html

4 Save the HTML document, then create a similar second document containing the same two hyperlinks
```
<a href="access.html" accesskey="1">Home Page</a> |
<a href="catalog.html" accesskey="2">Catalog Page</a>
```

5 Save the second HTML document, then create a style sheet to remove the default hyperlink styles and to highlight each hyperlink when they receive focus

```
a        { text-decoration : none ; color : black ; }
a:focus { background : red ; color : white ; }
```

access.css

6 Now, save the style sheet, then open the first web page in your browser to see the hyperlinks without default styles

Removing the default hyperlink styles means they are no longer easily recognizable as links – so it is best avoided unless some other indication makes the user aware they can be used for navigation purposes.

7 Hit the Tab key repeatedly until the second hyperlink receives focus, then hit Return to follow that link

Mac users should press CMD + *accesskey* with their Safari browser.

8 Press the appropriate access key combination for your browser and number 1 key, such as **ALT + 1**, then hit Return to follow the first hyperlink

Linking to page fragments

Hyperlinks can target a specific point in a document that has been created with a "fragment" identifier – an element with a unique identifying name assigned to an **id** attribute in its opening tag. Within the hyperlink, the fragment identifier is specified to a **href** attribute in the opening **<a>** tag prefixed by a # hash character. For example, the tag **<a href="#top">** targets an element within the same document that contains the unique fragment identifier name of "top".

A hyperlink can also target a specific point in a different document using the document's URL, followed by a # hash character, then the fragment identifier. For example, the tag **<a href="index.html#top">** targets an element within a document named "index.html" that contains the unique fragment identifier name of "top".

Following a hyperlink to a fragment identifier displays the document from the point where the fragment identifier appears:

The # hash character is used in HTML to target fragments and to specify hexadecimal color values, and in CSS to select elements by their **id** attribute for styling.

fragment.html

1 Start with the HTML5 document type declaration
<!DOCTYPE HTML>

2 Add a root element containing head and body sections, with a link element pointing to a style sheet
<html lang="en">
<head>
<meta charset="UTF-8">
<title>Fragment Example</title>
<link rel="stylesheet" href="fragment.css">
</head>
<body> <!-- Content to go here --> **</body>**
</html>

3 Within the body section, insert two hyperlinks that contain fragment identifiers and also target different fragments
<a id="top" href="#btm">Skip to Page Foot</a> |
<a id="next-btm" href="next.html#btm">
                    Skip to Next Page Foot</a>

4 Next, in the body, insert a content paragraph followed by a hyperlink containing a fragment identifier and targeting the first hyperlink in the document
<p class="yellow-block">Content...</p>
<a id="btm" href="#top">Skip to Page Head</a>

...cont'd

5 Save the HTML document, then create a second similar document with hyperlinks both above and below content

```
<a id="top" href="#btm">Skip to Page Foot</a>
<p class="red-block">Content...</p>
<a id="btm" href="#top">Skip to Page Head</a> |
<a id="prev-top" href="fragment.html#top">
                    Skip to Previous Page Head</a>
```

next.html

6 Create a style sheet that sizes and colors the content area of each document – representing different page bodies

```
p.yellow-block   { height : 700px ; background : yellow ; }
p.red-block       { height : 700px ; background : red ; }
```

fragment.css

7 Save the style sheet, then open the first web page in your browser and follow the hyperlinks to each of this document's fragments below and above its body content

8 Now, follow the hyperlink to the fragment in the second document, then return to the top of the first document

At the end of lengthy pages include a hyperlink to a fragment at the top of the page so the user need not scroll back up.

Linking to protocols

The **href** attribute of a hyperlink will typically target a resource using the HyperText Transfer protocol **http:** but it may also target resources using other protocols. Script functions can be called with the **javascript:** protocol, and email clients can be invoked by the **mailto:** protocol:

protocol.html

1 Start with the HTML5 document type declaration
`<!DOCTYPE HTML>`

2 Add a root element containing a head section, incorporating a style sheet and script, and a body section

```
<html lang="en">
<head>
<meta charset="UTF-8">
<title>Protocol Example</title>
<link rel="stylesheet" href="protocol.css">
<script src="protocol.js"></script>
</head>
<body>  <!-- Content to go here -->  </body>
</html>
```

3 Within the body section, insert an image and a paragraph containing two hyperlinks that target different protocols

```
<img id="chart" src="chart.png" alt="Chart Image">
<p id="links">
<a href="javascript:toggle()">Show/Hide Chart</a> <br>
<a href="mailto:wendy@example.com">Email Wendy</a>
</p>
```

protocol.css

4 Save the HTML document, then create a style sheet with a rule to hide the image and a rule to style the paragraph

```
img#chart { visibility : hidden ; height : 0px ; }
p#links { padding : 5px ;
          border : 3px double green ; width : 200px ; }
```

protocol.js

5 Save the style sheet, then create a script to alternately reveal and hide the image when the first hyperlink gets activated

```
function toggle()
{
  var tag = document.getElementById( "chart" ) ;
  var hid = ( tag.style.visibility !== "visible" ) ;
  tag.style.visibility = ( hid ) ? "visible" : "hidden" ;
  tag.style.height = ( hid ) ? "auto" : "0px" ;
}
```

6 Save the script, then open the web page in your browser and click on the first link to reveal the image element

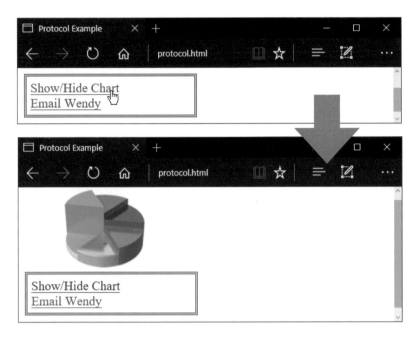

This script first examines the current visibility status of the image element, then reverses it.

73

7 Click on the first hyperlink to hide the image element again, then click on the second hyperlink to launch your default client email application – ready to send a message

Don't forget

The **mailto:** protocol automatically adds the email address of the recipient in the "To" field of the email client.

Using images as hyperlinks

To make the navigational features of an HTML document more visually appealing, images can be used as hyperlinks – simply by nesting an **<img>** element within an **<a>** hyperlink element:

rollover.html

1 Start with the HTML5 document type declaration
<!DOCTYPE HTML>

2 Add a root element containing head and body sections, with a link element pointing to a style sheet
<html lang="en">
<head>
<meta charset="UTF-8">
<title>Rollover Example</title>
<link rel="stylesheet" href="rollover.css">
</head>
<body> <!-- Content to go here --> **</body>**
</html>

3 Within the body section, insert a paragraph containing a hyperlink with a nested image of a specific size
<p class="btn">
<a href="http://www.youtube.com">
<img src="rollover-btn.png"
**   alt="Hyperlink to YouTube" width="192" height="67" >**
</a>
</p>

4 Save the HTML document, then open the web page in your browser and follow the hyperlink

Don't forget

The dimensions of this button are exaggerated for illustration purposes – web page buttons are typically smaller.

Browsers usually add a border around an image when it is nested within a hyperlink to indicate that it is not merely an illustration. Style rules can remove the image border and can also swap the image when the cursor is placed over it to perform a "rollover". There are several ways to achieve this effect – the technique described below hides the image when the cursor is placed over it, to reveal the background image on the container element behind:

5 Create a style sheet beginning with a rule to set the paragraph container element the same size as the button image and to specify the container's background image
p.btn { width : 192px ; height : 67px ;
     background : url(rollover-bg.png) ; }

rollover.css

6 Next, add a style rule to set the nested hyperlink element to the same size as the button image
p.btn a { display : block ; width : 192px ; height : 67px ; }

7 Now, add a style rule to remove the default border from around the nested button image element
p.btn a img { border : 0px ; }

Hot tip

8 Finally, add a style rule to hide the button image when the cursor is placed over it
p.btn a:hover img { visibility : hidden ; }

9 Save the style sheet then open the web page in your browser to see the border removed and the rollover effect

Unlike some other rollover techniques, here both images are already loaded, so the rollover performs instantly – and the **<img>** tag provides alternative text when images are disabled.

Producing image map links

A single image can target multiple hyperlink resources if an image "map" is added to define "hot spot" areas for each hyperlink. To use an image map, the **<img>** tag must include a **usemap** attribute to specify a map name, prefixed by a **#** hash character. The image map itself is contained between **<map> </map>** tags, and its name is specified by a **name** attribute in the opening **<map>** tag.

Each area of the image that is to become a hyperlink hot spot is defined by four attributes of an **<area>** tag within the **<map>** element. The **shape** attribute specifies its shape as **rect** (rectangle), **circle** or **poly** (polygon), and the **coords** attribute specifies a comma-separated list of its x-axis and y-axis coordinates:

Shape:	Coordinates:
rect	top-left x, top-left y, bottom-right x, bottom-right y
circle	center x, center y, radius
poly	x1,y1,x2,y2,x3,y3,etc. – one pair for each point. The first and final point must have identical coordinates to complete the shape

Additionally, each **<area>** tag must have an **href** attribute, to specify the hyperlink's URL target, and an **alt** attribute to specify alternative text to be displayed when images are not enabled.

map.html

1 Start with the HTML5 document type declaration
<!DOCTYPE HTML>

2 Add a root element containing head and body sections
<html lang="en">
<head>
<meta charset="UTF-8">
<title>Image Map Example</title>
</head>
<body> <!-- Content to go here --> **</body>**
</html>

3 Within the body section, insert an image and map element
<img src="search.png" alt="Search" usemap="#search">
<map name="search"> <!-- Areas to go here --> **</map>**

4 Within the map element, define a rectangular hot spot covering the top left quarter of the image – from a top left point at x,y:0,0 to a bottom right point at x,y:200,100

```
<area   shape="rect" coords="0,0,200,100"
        href="http://www.bing.com"
        alt="Bing Panel" title="Link to Bing">
```

5 Now, in the map element, define three hot spots of the same size covering the other three quarters of the image

```
<area   shape="rect" coords="200,0,400,100"
        href="http://www.ask.com"
        alt="Ask Panel" title="Link to Ask">

<area   shape="rect" coords="0,100,200,200"
        href="http://www.google.com"
        alt="Google Panel" title="Link to Google">

<area   shape="rect" coords="200,100,400,200"
        href="http://www.yahoo.com" alt="Yahoo Panel"
        title="Link to Yahoo">
```

6 Save the HTML document, then open the web page in your browser to see the tooltips describe each hot spot that you can follow to open its associated target resource

Do not leave any spaces in the comma-separated list of coordinates.

search.png
400px x 200px

Validation will fail unless each **<area>** tag includes an **alt** attribute.

77

Generating popups

Hyperlinks can also be used without an actual target resource to perform both CSS rollovers and "popup" effects. Typically, the hyperlink's **<a>** anchor tag **href** attribute will specify a **#null** value in this case. The CSS **a:hover** pseudo-class can create hot spots – much like the image map hot spots in the previous example. In response, the style rules can reveal previously hidden HTML elements to be displayed as popups in front of other content. These are useful to display additional graphical or text content:

popup.html

1 Start with the HTML5 document type declaration
```
<!DOCTYPE HTML>
```

2 Add a root element containing head and body sections, with a link element pointing to a style sheet
```
<html lang="en">
<head>
<meta charset="UTF-8">
<title>PopUp Example</title>
<link rel="stylesheet" href="popup.css">
</head>
<body>  <!-- Content to go here -->  </body>
</html>
```

Hot tip

Specifying a value of just "#" to a hyperlink's **href** attribute targets the top of that document.

3 Within the body section, insert a paragraph containing hyperlinks with nested image elements
```
<p id="models">
<a href="#null">Cayman
<img class="pop" src="cayman.png" alt="Cayman">
</a>

<a href="#null">Boxster
<img class="pop" src="boxster.png" alt="Boxster">
</a>

<a href="#null">Carrera
<img class="pop" src="carrera.png" alt="Carrera">
</a>
</p>
```

4 Next, in the body, insert a paragraph containing text
```
<p >
Porsche doesn't simply build sports cars.<br>Porsche is
more. Much more. And Porsche is different.
</p>
```

5 Save the HTML document, then create a style sheet that removes browser defaults and initially hides the images
```
* { margin : 0 ; padding : 0 ; border : 0 ; }
img.pop
{ position : absolute ; top : 20px ; left : 190px ;
padding : 15px ; visibility : hidden ; height : 0px ; }
```

popup.css

6 Next, add rules to size and position both paragraphs
```
p { width : 150px ; float : left ; margin : 20px 0 0 20px ; }
```

7 Now, add rules to style the hyperlinks
```
p#models a
{ display : block ; padding : 5px ; margin : 0 0 20px 0 ;
color : white ; background : blue ; text-decoration : none ; }

p#models a:hover { color : #FFF ; background : #F00 ; }

p#models a:hover  img.pop
{ border : 5px solid red ; background : #FFF ;
z-index : 10 ; visibility : visible ; height : auto ; }
```

Don't forget

Notice that the foreground and background colors for the hyperlink's hover state are specified using hexadecimal shorthand values for red and white.

8 Save the style sheet, then open the web page in your browser and place the cursor over any hyperlink to see its associated image appear above the text paragraph

Summary

- The HTML5 **<a> </a>** anchor tags are used to enclose hyperlinks within an HTML document.

- An **href** attribute can be included in an **<a>** anchor tag to specify the URL of a target resource for that hyperlink.

- Each hyperlink is sensitive to hover, active and visited states.

- Hyperlinks can be accessed by a pointer, the tab key or a designated key specified by the **<a>** tag's **accesskey** attribute.

- An **id** attribute can be included in an element to create a fragment identifier that can become the target of a hyperlink.

- When targeting a fragment, the hyperlink's **href** attribute must specify the identifier name prefixed by a **#** hash character.

- A hyperlink may target a resource via the **http:** protocol, or with other protocols such as **javascript:** and **mailto:**.

- Rollover effects are performed by the CSS **a:hover** pseudo-class to swap images in response to cursor position.

- A single image can target multiple hyperlink resources by adding an image map to specify an area for each hyperlink.

- The **<map> </map>** tags enclose **<area>** elements, to define the areas of an image map, and a **name** attribute must be included in the **<map>** tag to specify a name for that map.

- To use an image map, the **<img>** tag must include a **usemap** attribute specifying the map's name prefixed by a **#** hash character.

- Each **<area>** tag must include **shape, coords, href** and **alt** attributes and the shape may be a value of **rect, circle** or **poly**.

- Hyperlinks can be used without resource targets to perform CSS effects by assigning a **#null** value to the **<a>** tag's **href** attribute.

- Popup effects can be performed by the CSS **a:hover** pseudo-class to reveal hidden content in response to cursor position.

5

Arranging content sections

This chapter demonstrates how to group content into sections within the body of an HTML5 document.

82 Proclaiming headings

84 Grouping headers

86 Providing navigation

88 Writing articles

90 Standing aside

92 Footing the page

94 Positioning content

96 Denying anonymity

98 Summary

Proclaiming headings

HTML5 heading elements are created using **<h1>**, **<h2>**, **<h3>**, **<h4>**, **<h5>**, and **<h6>** tags. These are ranked in importance by their numeric value – where **<h1>** has the greatest importance, and **<h6>** has the least importance. Each heading requires a matching closing tag and should only contain heading text. Typically, the heading's font size and weight will reflect its importance, but headings also serve other purposes.

Heading elements should be used to implicitly convey the document structure by correctly sequencing them – so **<h2>** elements below a **<h1>** element, **<h3>** elements below a **<h2>** element, and so on. This structure helps readers quickly skim through a document by navigating its headings. Search engine spiders may promote documents that have correctly sequenced headings as they can use the headings in their index. They assume headings are likely to describe their content so it is especially useful to include meta keywords from the document's head section in the document's headings.

The **<h1>** element is by far the most important heading and should ideally appear only once to proclaim the document heading. Often this can be a succinct version of the document title. Below that, a number of **<h2>** headings can proclaim section headings for long documents. Each section might contain individual article headings within **<h3>** elements, followed by paragraph **<p>** elements containing the actual article content.

heading.html

1 Start with the HTML5 document type declaration
<!DOCTYPE HTML>

2 Add a root element containing head and body sections
<html lang="en">
<head>
<meta charset="UTF-8"><title>Heading Example</title>
</head>
<body> **<!-- Content to go here -->** **</body>**
</html>

3 Within the body section, insert a main document heading
<h1>Document Heading</h1>

4 Next, within the body section, insert a section heading
<h2>Section Heading</h2>

5 Now, within the body section, insert some article headings followed by paragraphs containing the article content
```
<h3>Article Heading</h3> <p>Article content...</p>
<h3>Article Heading</h3> <p>Article content...</p>
```

6 Finally, add another section with two more articles
```
<h2>Section Heading</h2>
<h3>Article Heading</h3> <p>Article content...</p>
<h3>Article Heading</h3> <p>Article content...</p>
```

7 Save the HTML document, then open it in your web browser to see the headings and document structure

Beware

Never use heading elements for their font properties as these can be overridden by style sheet rules – always consider headings to represent structure.

Hot tip

All screenshots throughout this chapter have added (unlisted) colored border styles to more clearly illustrate the page area occupied by the elements described.

The document structure created by the sequenced headings is known as the document "outline". Properly constructed outlines allow a part of the page, such as a single article, to be easily syndicated into another site. The outline for the document above is illustrated alongside.

1. Document Heading
   1. Section Heading
      1. Article Heading
      2. Article Heading
   2. Section Heading
      1. Article Heading
      2. Article Heading

83

Grouping headers

Headings sometimes have a sub-heading or tagline. For example, a document heading could be marked up like this:

```
<h1>American Airlines</h1>
<h2>Doing What We Do Best</h2>
```

Unfortunately, this would strictly require all subsequent headings to be **<h3>** down to **<h6>** – to maintain a correctly sequenced outline. Fortunately, HTML5 provides a grouping solution with the **<header> </header>** element. This can be used to enclose both the heading and sub-heading, like this:

```
<header>
<h1>American Airlines</h1>
<h2>Doing What We Do Best</h2>
</header>
```

Each document may contain multiple **<header>** elements, and each **<header>** element may contain headings **<h1>** down to **<h6>**. Complete headers may be enclosed in **<header> </header>** tags to include one or more headings along with other introductory items – such as a banner, logo, or a section's table of contents. Typically, a **<header>** element will contain the document heading at the start of a page, but may also be used at the start of sections within a page to contain associated introductory items.

header.html

1   Start with the HTML5 document type declaration **<!DOCTYPE HTML>**

2   Add a root element containing head and body sections
```
<html lang="en">
<head>
<meta charset="UTF-8">
<title>Header Example</title>
</head>
<body>  <!-- Content to go here -->  </body>
</html>
```

3   Within the body section, insert a main document heading
```
<header>

<!-- Banner image to go here -->

<h1>HTML5</h1>
<h2>Building better websites</h2>
</header>
```

...cont'd

4 Next, within the body section, insert a section and article
```
<h2>Section Heading</h2>
<h3>Article Heading</h3> <p> Article Content...</p>
```

5 Now, within the body section, insert a second section with a single article
```
<header>
<h1>CSS</h1> <h2>Cascading Style Sheets</h2>
</header>
<h3>Article Heading</h3> <p>Article content...</p>
```

6 Finally, insert a logo into the main document heading
```
<header>
<img src="banner.png" width="550"
        height="72" alt="Banner">
<h1>HTML5</h1>
<h2>Building better websites</h2>
</header>
```

7 Save the HTML document, then open it in your web browser to see the grouped headings and document header

Hot tip

The **<header>** element is not required for headings in a simple document – it is only needed to group together multiple items.

Don't forget

You cannot nest **<header>** elements, one within another, or place them within a page footer – see page 92.

1. HTML5
　　　1. Building better websites
　　　2. Section Heading
　　　　　1. Article Heading
2. CSS
　　　1. Cascading Style Sheets
　　　　　1. Article Heading

Providing navigation

Groups of hyperlinks on an HTML5 web page, which enable the user to navigate around the page or website, should be enclosed between **<nav> </nav>** tags. This may typically be a horizontal menu in the document header, or a vertical menu down the edge of the page. Note that the **<nav>** element is simply a wrapper around the menu – it does not replace any structural elements.

nav.html

Beware

Not every group of hyperlinks is eligible to be contained in a **<nav>** element – only those that provide page-wide or site-wide navigation.

1 Start with the HTML5 document type declaration
<!DOCTYPE HTML>

2 Add a root element containing head and body sections, with a link element pointing to a style sheet
```
<html lang="en">
<head>
<meta charset="UTF-8">
<title>Navigation Example</title>
<link rel="stylesheet" href="nav.css">
</head>
<body>  <!-- Content to go here -->  </body>
</html>
```

3 Within the body, insert a header containing a logo, document heading, and horizontal page navigation menu
```
<header>
<img id="logo" src="logo.png" alt="Logo">
<h1>Building better websites</h1>
<nav id="horizontal">
<p>
<a href="#html">Markup</a> |
<a href="#js">Scripting</a> |
<a href="#css">Style Sheets</a> </p>
</nav>
</header>
```

4 Next, in the body, insert a vertical site navigation menu
```
<nav id="vertical" >
<p>Further Reading<br>In Easy Steps:
<br><br> <a href="js.html">JavaScript</a>
<br><br> <a href="css.html">CSS</a> </p>
</nav>
```

5 Now, add regular content then save the HTML document
```
<h2 id="html">HTML5</h2> <p>All about markup...</p>
<h2 id="js">JavaScript</h2><p>All about scripting...</p>
<h2 id="css" >CSS</h2> <p>All about stylesheets...</p>
```

6 Create a style sheet to position the logo image and navigation menus

```
#logo    { float : left ; }
#horizontal      { padding-left : 100px ; display : block ; }
#vertical { float : left ; padding : 0px 30px 130px 30px ; }
```

nav.css

7 Save the HTML document and style sheet, then open the web page in your browser and try out the navigation links

Hot tip

It is popular to create vertical navigation menus as unordered lists – see ahead on page 100.

Remember that an **<article>** contains a stand-alone composition, but a **<section>** is just a grouping element.

section.html

Writing articles

In HTML5, all content within the **<body>** element is considered to be part of a "section". Within the main section, defined by the **<body>** element, section limits are defined implicitly by correctly sequenced headings in the document outline. Section limits may also be defined explicitly by placing content within the **<header>**, **<nav>**, **<section>** and **<article>** elements, plus the **<aside>**, and **<footer>** elements demonstrated over the next few pages.

General content within the document body, which is not part of a special content element such as **<nav>**, can be arranged in sections between **<section> </section>** tags. Each section will typically begin with its own heading element, followed by articles.

Each article should be enclosed between **<article> </article>** tags and will typically begin with its own heading element followed by one or more paragraphs.

In understanding the **<section>** and **<article>** elements, it helps to consider the way a newspaper contains various sections – news, sport, real estate, and so on. Each section contains various articles.

1 Start with the HTML5 document type declaration
<!DOCTYPE HTML>

2 Add a root element containing head and body sections
<html lang="en">
<head>
<meta charset="UTF-8">
<title>Section Example**</title>**
</head>
<body> <!-- Content to go here --> **</body>**
</html>

3 Within the body, insert a main document heading
<h1>Newspaper**</h1>**

4 Next, in the body, insert two section elements
<section>
<!-- Articles to go here -->
</section>

<section>
<!-- Articles to go here -->
</section>

5 Within the first section element, insert a section heading
`<h2>News Section</h2>`

6 Now, insert a section heading in the second section element
`<h2>Sport Section</h2>`

7 After the heading in each section, add two articles that
each contain an article heading and a single paragraph
```
<article>
<h3>Article #1</h3>
<p>Article content...</p>
</article>

<article>
<h3>Article #2</h3>
<p>Article content...</p>
</article>
```

8 Save the HTML document, then open it in your browser
to see the article content displayed in sections

A lengthy **<article>**
could even contain
nested **<section>**
elements, each
containing nested
<article> elements.

The document, section,
and article headings
appear correctly nested
in the document outline.

1. Newspaper
   1. News Section
      1. Article #1
      2. Article #2
   2. Sport Section
      1. Article #1
      2. Article #2

Standing aside

HTML5 usefully provides **<aside>** **</aside>** tags that can be nested within an **<article>** element in order to incorporate content that is somewhat related to the main content of that article. These allow for supplemental, yet separate, content to be included – typically displayed as a sidebar or footnote.

Content within an **<aside>** element should be stand-alone information that is related to the article, such as pull-quotes extracted from an affiliated article, a glossary of terms used within the article, or even hyperlinks to pages providing further reading associated with the article.

Alternatively, the **<aside>** element can be used alone, without an **<article>** element, to contain secondary content that is related to the entire page, such as related advertising or a blogroll.

aside.html

90

1. Start with the HTML5 document type declaration
<!DOCTYPE HTML>

2. Add a root element containing head and body sections, with a link element pointing to a style sheet
<html lang="en">
<head>
<meta charset="UTF-8">
<title>Aside Example</title>
<link rel="stylesheet" href="aside.css">
</head>
<body> <!-- Content to go here --> **</body>**
</html>

Hot tip

Avoid using the **<aside>** element to contain unrelated advertising.

3. Within the body, insert a main document heading
<h1>Famous Quotes</h1>

4. Next, within the body, insert an article containing a heading, a paragraph, and an aside element
<article>
<h2>Cynicism</h2>
**<p> <q>A cynic is a man who knows the price of everything
but the value of nothing.</q>
**
<cite>Oscar Wilde</cite>
</p>
**<aside>Oscar Wilde (1854 – 1900)
**
was an Irish writer and poet.</aside>
</article>

5 Now, within the body, insert a second article containing a heading, a paragraph, and an aside element

```
<article>
<h2>Happiness</h2>
<p><q>The secret of happiness is not in doing what one
likes, but in liking what one has to do.</q> <br>
<cite>James M. Barrie</cite>
</p>
<aside>James M. Barrie (1860 - 1937) was a Scottish
author and dramatist.</aside>
</article>
```

6 Insert an attribute into the opening tag of the first article element so it can be selected for sidebar styling

```
<article class="sidebar">
```

7 Create a style sheet to control the position of the paragraph and aside element in the first article

```
article.sidebar > p,aside
{ display : table-cell ; padding-right: 20px ; }
```

aside.css

8 Save the HTML document and the style sheet, then open the web page in your browser to see how the asides appear

Do not use the **<aside>** element to contain navigation hyperlinks – those should always be contained inside a **<nav>** element.

Footing the page

Just as each HTML5 document may contain multiple headings, for the document, sections and articles, they may also contain multiple footers for the document, sections and articles. The content of each footer is contained between **<footer> </footer>** tags and provides information about that part of the document.

Typically, a **<footer>** element might contain the author's name, the author's contact details within an **<address>** element, or copyright and legal disclaimers within a **<small>** element.

Like a **<header>** element, a **<footer>** element can also contain hyperlinks for page and site navigation within a nested **<nav>** element. Hyperlinks to related documents, however, are better placed in an **<aside>** element within the section or article.

footer.html

1 Start with the HTML5 document type declaration
<!DOCTYPE HTML>

2 Add a root element containing head and body sections, with a link element pointing to a style sheet
<html lang="en">
<head>
<meta charset="UTF-8">
<title>Footer Example</title>
<link rel="stylesheet" href="footer.css">
</head>
<body> <!-- Content to go here --> **</body>**
</html>

3 Within the body, insert a main document heading
<h1 id="top">Interesting Articles</h1>

The HTML5 **<aside>** and **<nav>** elements may also each contain a **<footer>** element.

4 Next, within the body, just before its closing tag, insert a document footer containing page navigation hyperlinks
<footer id="page">
<nav>
<a href="#art-1">Sally's Article</a> -
<a href="#art-2">Terry's Article</a> -
<a href="#top">Top of Page</a>
</nav>
</footer>

5 Next, within the document footer, insert copyright details
<small>Copyright © Example Corporation</small>

6 Now, within the body, between the document heading and document footer, insert two articles that each contain an article heading, a paragraph, and an article footer

```
<article>
<h2 id="art-1">Sally's Article</h2>
<p>Article content...</p>
<footer>
<address>sally@example.com</address>
</footer>
</article>

<article>
<h2 id="art-2">Terry's Article</h2>
<p>Article content...</p>
<footer>
<address>terry@example.com</address>
</footer>
</article>
```

7 Create a style sheet to control the position of the page footer contents

```
footer#page { margin-top : 20px ; }
```

footer.css

8 Save the HTML document and the style sheet, then open the web page in your browser to see how the footers appear

<section> elements are not required in short documents like this one – unless you particularly want to add section headings and footers.

Positioning content

Just as HTML provides a **<header>** element to group together related items at the top of the page, and a **<footer>** element to group together related items at the bottom of the page, it also provides a **<main>** element to group together related items that form the body content of the page. A **<main>** element can contain any kind of content that is not related to the page header or footer information. For example, sections, articles, paragraphs, sidebar notes, images, etc.

Using the **<main>** element in combination with the elements introduced throughout this chapter, the document header, main content and footer can be positioned in a logical structure:

position.html

1 Start with the HTML5 document type declaration
<!DOCTYPE HTML>

2 Add a root element containing head and body sections, with a link element pointing to a style sheet
```
<html lang="en">
<head>
<meta charset="UTF-8">
<title>Position Example</title>
<link rel="stylesheet" href="position.css">
</head>
<body>  <!-- Content to go here -->  </body>
</html>
```

3 Within the body, insert a document header
```
<header>Header Area<br><h1>Document Heading</h1>
<nav>Navigation Area</nav></header>
```

4 Next, within the body, insert the main content element
```
<main>Main Area<br>
<!-- Sections to go here -->
</main>
```

5 Now, within the main content element, insert two sections
```
<section><h2>Section Heading</h2>
<!-- Articles to go here -->
</section>

<section><h2>Section Heading</h2>
<!-- Articles to go here -->
</section>
```

6 Then within each section, insert two articles
`<article><h3>`**Article Heading**`</h3>`
`<p>`**Paragraph**`</p>` `<p>`**Paragraph**`</p>`
`</article>`

`<article><h3>`**Article Heading**`</h3>`
`<p>`**Paragraph**`</p>` `<p>`**Paragraph**`</p>`
`</article>`

7 Finally, within the body, insert a document footer
`<footer><h2>`**Footer Area**`</h2></footer>`

8 Create the style sheet to add borders and color to each element, then save the HTML document and style sheet and open the page in your browser to see the structure

position.css
(unlisted)

Always use white page backgrounds, as colored backgrounds can make content difficult to read.

1. Document Heading
   1. Navigation Area
   2. Section Heading
      1. Article Heading
      2. Article Heading
   3. Section Heading
      1. Article Heading
      2. Article Heading
   4. Footer Area

Only use the **<div>** element as a last resort, because it has no meaning – always look for a meaningful element to use instead.

96

division.html
(original body section)

Denying anonymity

The dividing **<div> </div>** tags, which were used widely in earlier versions of HTML, continue to be supported in HTML5 for backward-compatibility – but the **<div>** element should only now be used as a last resort, when no other element is suitable. Unlike other meaningful elements such as **<header>**, **<main>**, **<section>**, **<article>**, **<nav>** and **<footer>**, the meaningless **<div>** element is anonymous. For example, a smart browser might have a shortcut key to jump to the page's navigation section. This section is easily identifiable when contained in a meaningful **<nav>** element, but not so when contained in a meaningless **<div>** element.

The **<div>** element remains useful for styling purposes, as do the similarly anonymous **<span> </span>** tags. Although the **<div>** and **<span>** elements are meaningless alone, they can include an identifying attribute to wrap content that is to be styled alike.

Documents that use the **<div>** element for structural, rather than stylistic purposes should be edited to use meaningful elements instead. For example, given the body section elements below:

```
<div class="header">
<h1>Web Languages</h1>
</div>

<div class="nav">
<h2>Menu</h2>
<p><a href="js.html">JavaScript</a></p>
<p><a href="css.html">Cascading Style Sheets</a></p>
</div>

<div class="main">
<h2>HyperText <span>Markup</span> Language</h2>
<p>All about HTML...</p>

<h2>eXtensible <span>Markup</span> Language</h2>
<p>All about XML...</p>
</div>

<div class="footer">
<p><small>Copyright &copy; Example Corporation</small></p>
</div>
```

It should hopefully be obvious from these class attribute values that each anonymous **<div>** element can be easily replaced by more meaningful **<header>**, **<nav>**, **<main>** and **<footer>** elements.

…cont'd

1 Replace the "header" class **<div>** with a **<header>** element
<header> <h1>Web Languages</h1> </header>

2 Replace the "nav" class **<div>** with a **<nav>** element
<nav> <h2>Menu</h2>
<p><a href="js.html">JavaScript</a></p>
<p><a href="css.html">Cascading Style Sheets</a></p>
</nav>

3 Replace the "main" class **<div>** with **<main>** and
<article> elements
<main> <article>
<h2>HyperText <span>Markup</span> Language</h2>
<p>All about HTML...</p> </article>
<article>
<h2>eXtensible <span>Markup</span> Language</h2>
<p>All about XML...</p> </article> </main>

4 Replace the "footer" class **<div>** with a **<footer>** element
<footer> <p>
<small>Copyright © Example Corporation</small>
</p> </footer>

5 Save the document, then open it in your browser to see it
appears the same – but it now has meaningful structure

division.html
(body section revision)

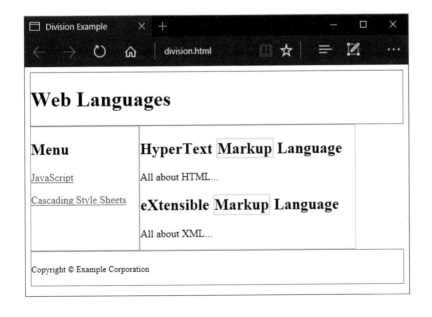

Also amend any
associated style sheet to
select the new elements.

Summary

- Heading elements **<h1>**, **<h2>**, **<h3>**, **<h4>**, **<h5>** and **<h6>** are ranked in order of importance from **<h1>** down to **<h6>**.

- Correctly sequenced heading elements implicitly convey the document structure, to create the document outline.

- Complete headers, including a logo and headings **<h1>** to **<h6>** can be enclosed in a **<header>** element.

- Groups of hyperlinks providing page or site navigation should be enclosed within a **<nav>** element.

- A **<nav>** element is just a wrapper around a menu, typically displayed horizontally in the header or vertically in a sidebar.

- Section limits are explicitly defined in a document outline when content is placed within **<header>**, **<nav>**, **<section>**, **<article>**, **<aside>** and **<footer>** elements.

- Each document **<section>** element will typically begin with a section heading, followed by one or more articles.

- Each document **<article>** element will typically begin with an article heading, followed by one or more paragraphs.

- Stand-alone information related to an article can be enclosed within an **<aside>** element nested in an **<article>** element.

- Typically, a **<footer>** element might contain contact details in an **<address>** element or legal details in a **<small>** element.

- A **<main>** element can be used as a wrapper around all body content that is not related to header or footer information.

- The anonymous **<div>** and **<span>** elements are best avoided for structural purposes, but are useful for styling purposes.

6

Writing lists and tables

This chapter demonstrates how to create lists and tables in the body section of an HTML5 document.

100 Creating unordered lists

102 Creating ordered lists

104 Creating definition lists

106 Producing a simple table

108 Spanning cells over rows

110 Spanning cells across columns

112 Adding a header and footer

114 Aligning cell content

116 Grouping columns

118 Setting column widths

120 Utilizing templates

122 Summary

Creating unordered lists

Unordered lists, where the sequence of list items is not important, typically place a bullet-point before each item to differentiate list items from regular text.

In HTML5, unordered lists are created with **<ul> </ul>** tags, which provide a container for list items. Each list item can be created using **<li> </li>** tags to enclose the item, or optionally just using **<li>** to precede the item – either form of **<li>** element validates as correct HTML. An unordered list **<ul>** element can contain numerous list item **<li>** elements.

The bullet point that differentiates unordered list items from regular text may be one of these three marker types:

- **Disc** – a filled circular bullet-point (the default style).

- **Circle** – an unfilled circular bullet-point.

- **Square** – a filled square bullet-point.

A style rule can specify any one of the above values to the unordered list's **list-style-type** property, or a **none** value can be specified to that property to suppress bullet-points.

Each HTML list also has a **list-style-image** property that can specify the URL of an image to be used as the list's bullet-point. This will appear in place of any of the marker type bullet-points. Where the web browser cannot use the specified image, the marker specified to its **list-style-type** property will be used, or when no marker has been specified, the default will be used.

ulist.html

1 Start with the HTML5 document type declaration
<!DOCTYPE HTML>

2 Add a root element containing head and body sections, with a link element pointing to a style sheet
<html lang="en">
<head>
<meta charset="UTF-8">
<title>Unordered List Example</title>
<link rel="stylesheet" href="ulist.css">
</head>
<body> <!-- Content to go here --> **</body>**
</html>

3 Within the body section, insert four copies of this complete unordered list, with no specified class name

```
<ul class="">
<li>JavaScript</li>
<li>Cascading Style Sheets</li>
<li>C Programming</li> </ul>
```

Hot tip

Note that in CSS terms, the lists are written in a content box with their bullet-points drawn in its left padding area.

4 Now, edit each list in turn to provide a class name

```
<ul class=" disc-bullets">
<ul class=" circle-bullets">
<ul class=" square-bullets">
<ul class=" image-bullets">
```

5 Next, make the final list into a site navigation menu, by enclosing it within a **<nav>** element and making each list item into a hyperlink

```
<nav> <ul class=" image-bullets">
<li><a href="script.html">JavaScript</a></li>
<li><a href="style.html">Cascading Style Sheets</a></li>
<li><a href="program.html">C Programming</a></li>
</ul> </nav>
```

6 Create a style sheet to position each list and to specify their individual bullet-point styles

```
ul.disc-bullets    { list-style-type : disc ; float : left ; }
ul.circle-bullets  { list-style-type : circle ; float : left ; }
ul.square-bullets  { list-style-type : square ; float : left ; }
ul.image-bullets   { list-style-image : url( go.png ) ; clear :
both ; }
```

ulist.css

7 Save the HTML document and style sheet, then open the web page in your browser to see the list bullet points

go.png 21px x 21px

Creating ordered lists

Ordered lists, where the sequence of list items is important, number each item to differentiate list items from regular text.

In HTML5, ordered lists are created with **<ol> </ol>** tags, which provide a container for list items. As with unordered lists, each list item can be created using **<li> </li>** tags to enclose the item, or optionally just using **<li>** to precede the item – either form of **<li>** element validates as correct HTML. An ordered list **<ol>** element can contain numerous list item **<li>** elements.

The automatic numbering that differentiates ordered list items from regular text may be one of these six numbering types:

- **Decimal** – traditional numerals (the default style).

- **Roman** – classical numerals.

- **Latin** – traditional alphabetical lettering.

- **Greek** – classical alphabetical lettering.

- **Georgian** – traditional Georgian numbering.

- **Armenian** – traditional Armenian numbering.

A style rule can specify any of the above numbering types to the list's **list-style-type** property with the following values:

Type:	Value:
Decimal	**decimal** or **decimal-leading-zero**
Roman	**lower-roman** or **upper-roman**
Latin	**lower-latin** or **upper-latin** **lower-alpha** or **upper-alpha**
Greek	**lower-greek**
Georgian	**georgian**
Armenian	**armenian**

Additionally, a **none** value can be specified to suppress numbering. List item numbering will normally begin at one, but a different start point can be specified to a **start** attribute in the **<ol>** tag.

When no numbering type has been specified, the default will be used.

As with the markers in unordered lists, numbering is drawn in the left padding area of the list's content box.

1 Start with the HTML5 document type declaration
`<!DOCTYPE HTML>`

olist.html

2 Add a root element containing head and body sections, with a link element pointing to a style sheet
```
<html lang="en">
<head>
<meta charset="UTF-8">
<title>Ordered List Example</title>
<link rel="stylesheet" href="olist.css">
</head>
<body> <!-- Content to go here --> </body>
</html>
```

3 Within the body section, insert three ordered lists
```
<ol id="list-1">
<li>Cheetah<li>Pronghorn Antelope<li>Blue Wildebeest</li>
</ol>
<ol id="list-2">
<li>Lion<li>Springbok<li>Brown Hare</li>
</ol>
<ol id="list-3">
<li>Nile<li>Amazon<li>Mississippi</li>
</ol>
```

4 Now, edit the second list to begin numbering at four
`<ol id="list-2" start="4">`

5 Create a style sheet to position the lists and to specify how the items should be numbered
```
ol { display : table-cell ; }
ol#list-2 { padding-right : 20px ; }
ol#list-3 { list-style-type : upper-roman ;
padding-left : 50px ; border-left : 3px dashed black ; }
```

olist.css

6 Save the HTML document and style sheet, then open the web page in your browser to see the list numbering

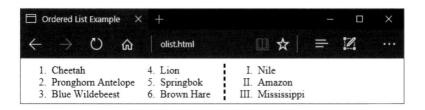

Creating definition lists

A definition list is a unique type of list in which each list item has two parts – the first part being a term, and the second part being a description of the term in the first part. This is referred to as a name/value pair. For example, a name/value pair for the term "sun" could be "sun/the star at the center of our solar system".

In HTML5, definition lists are created with **<dl> </dl>** tags, which provide a container for list items. Each list item term is contained between **<dt> </dt>** definition term tags, and each list item description is contained between **<dd> </dd>** definition description tags. Optionally, the **</dt>** and **</dd>** closing tags may be omitted – either form of **<dt>** and **<dd>** element is valid.

Each list item in a definition list can contain multiple **<dt>** definition term elements and multiple **<dd>** definition description elements – to allow a single term to have multiple descriptions, or multiple terms to have a single description. Typically, browsers display the definition descriptions inset from their terms.

Definition lists are also useful to contain a series of questions and related answers, or indeed any other groups of name/value data.

dlist.html

1 Start with the HTML5 document type declaration
```
<!DOCTYPE HTML>
```

2 Add a root element containing head and body sections, with a link element pointing to a style sheet
```
<html lang="en">
<head>
<meta charset="UTF-8">
<title>Definition List Example</title>
<link rel="stylesheet" href="dlist.css">
</head>
<body>  <!-- Content to go here -->  </body>
</html>
```

3 Within the body section, insert a definition list containing two question and answer name/value pairs
```
<dl>
  <dt>What is HTML5?</dt>
  <dd>The latest HyperText Markup Language</dd>

  <dt>When can I use it?</dt>
  <dd>Right now.</dd>
</dl>
```

4 Next, in the body section, insert a second definition list containing two list items that each have multiple descriptions – describing the use, pronunciation, and meaning of their term

```
<dl>
<dt><dfn>Homonym</dfn></dt>
<dd class="grammar">noun</dd>
<dd class="spoken">[hom-uh-nim]</dd>
<dd>a word the same as another in sound and spelling
but different in meaning</dd>

<dt><dfn>Mouse</dfn></dt>
<dd class="grammar">noun</dd>
<dd class="spoken">[mous]</dd>
<dd>a small animal of various rodent families</dd>
<dd>a palm-sized button-operated device used to move a
computer cursor</dd> <dd>a quiet, timid person</dd>
</dl>
```

The **<dt>** element alone does not indicate that its content is a term being defined – a nested **<dfn>** element must be used for that purpose.

5 Create a style sheet to color the question and definition terms in the lists, and to color some specific descriptions

```
dt { color : blue ; }
dfn { color : red ; font-size : 20pt ; }
dd.grammar { color : green ; }
dd.spoken { color : blue ; }
```

dlist.css

6 Save the HTML document and style sheet, then open the web page in your browser to see the name/value pairs

Do not use a definition list to mark up dialog – use paragraphs to mark up each piece of dialog instead.

105

Hot tip

Omit the closing **</td>** cell tags but include the closing **</tr>** tags to more clearly denote the end of each table row.

table.html

Producing a simple table

Data is often best presented in tabular form, arranged in rows and columns to logically group related items, so it is easily understood.

In HTML5, tables are created with **<table> </table>** tags, which provide a container for table rows. Each table row is created with **<tr> </tr>** tags, which provide a container for a line of table data cells. Each table data cell is created with **<td> </td>** tags, which enclose the actual data to be presented. Optionally, the **</td>** and **</tr>** closing tags may be omitted – either form of **<td>** and **<tr>** element is valid.

A **<table>** element will typically contain numerous **<tr>** elements to create a table displaying multiple rows of data. Similarly, each **<tr>** element will typically contain numerous **<td>** elements to create a table of multiple columns of data. It is important to note, however, that each **<tr>** row in the table must contain the exact same number of **<td>** cells – so, for example, if the first **<tr>** row contains five **<td>** cells, all **<tr>** rows must contain five **<td>** cells.

1 Start with the HTML5 document type declaration
<!DOCTYPE HTML>

2 Add a root element containing head and body sections, with a link element pointing to a style sheet
<html lang="en">
<head>
<meta charset="UTF-8">
<title>Table Example</title>
<link rel="stylesheet" href="table.css">
</head>
<body> <!-- Content to go here --> **</body>**
</html>

3 Within the body section, insert a table element that includes an identity for styling purposes
<table id="data">
<!-- Table rows to go here -->
</table>

4 Now, within the table element, insert three rows that each contain three table data cells
<tr> <td>Cell 1.1 <td>Cell 1.2 <td>Cell 1.3 </tr>
<tr> <td>Cell 2.1 <td>Cell 2.2 <td>Cell 2.3 </tr>
<tr> <td>Cell 3.1 <td>Cell 3.2 <td>Cell 3.3 </tr>

5 Create a style sheet to set the table width and font, and also to add borders to the table, its cells, and its headings (added later below)

table#data { width : 580px ; font-family : sans-serif ; border : 5px solid black ; }
table#data td,th { border : 1px solid black ; }

table.css

6 Save the HTML document and style sheet, then open the web page to see this simple table

If a **<caption>**: element is to be included, it must immediately follow the opening **<table>** tag.

Cell 1.1	Cell 1.2	Cell 1.3
Cell 2.1	Cell 2.2	Cell 2.3
Cell 3.1	Cell 3.2	Cell 3.3

A table title can be specified with **<caption> </caption>** tags and row and column headings can be added between **<th> </th>** tags.

7 Immediately following the opening table tag, insert a caption title and a new row of four column headings

<caption>A Simple Table</caption>
<tr><th><th>Column 1<th>Column 2<th>Column 3</tr>

The closing **</th>** tag is optional but the number of opening **<th>** headings must exactly match the number of rows and columns.

8 Finally, insert a row heading at the start of each following row, then save the HTML document to view the additions

<tr><th>Row 1<td>Cell 1.1<td>Cell 1.2<td>Cell 1.3</tr>
<tr><th>Row 2<td>Cell 2.1<td>Cell 2.2<td>Cell 2.3</tr>
<tr><th>Row 3<td>Cell 3.1<td>Cell 3.2<td>Cell 3.3</tr>

A Simple Table

	Column 1	Column 2	Column 3
Row 1	Cell 1.1	Cell 1.2	Cell 1.3
Row 2	Cell 2.1	Cell 2.2	Cell 2.3
Row 3	Cell 3.1	Cell 3.2	Cell 3.3

Subsequent examples in this chapter build upon this simple table example as more table features are introduced.

Spanning cells over rows

An individual table cell can be combined with others vertically to span down over multiple rows of a table. The number of rows to be spanned is specified to a **rowspan** attribute in the spanning cell's **<td>** tag. Cells in the rows being spanned must then be removed to maintain the table symmetry.

rowspan.html

1 Make a copy of the **table.html** document, created in the previous example, and rename it "rowspan.html"

2 Change the document and table titles
<title>Row Spanning Example</title>
<caption>A Table Spanning Rows</caption>

3 In the table data element containing the text "Cell 1.1", insert an attribute in its opening tag and edit its content
<td rowspan="2">Cell 1.1+2.1</td>

4 Now, delete the table data element containing the text "Cell 2.1" – as this cell is now spanned

table.css
(additions)

5 Save the HTML document, then re-open the **table.css** style sheet and add rules to style cells spanning rows
table#data td[rowspan="2"] { background : yellow ; }
table#data td[rowspan="3"] { background : aqua ; }

6 Save the style sheet then open the web page in your browser to see the cell spanning two rows in Column 1

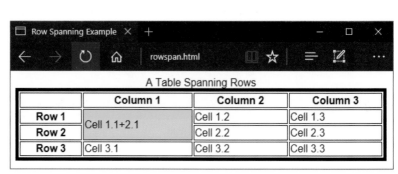

	Column 1	Column 2	Column 3
Row 1	Cell 1.1+2.1	Cell 1.2	Cell 1.3
Row 2		Cell 2.2	Cell 2.3
Row 3	Cell 3.1	Cell 3.2	Cell 3.3

7 Reopen the HTML document, then insert an attribute into the table data element containing the text "Cell 2.2" and edit its content
`<td rowspan="2">Cell 2.2+3.2</td>`

Hot tip

Insert tab spaces between all table data elements in the HTML code to align them so it's easier to configure the table layout.

8 Now, delete the table data element containing the text "Cell 3.2" – as this cell is now spanned

9 Save the amended HTML document, then open it in your browser to see the cell spanning two rows in Column 2

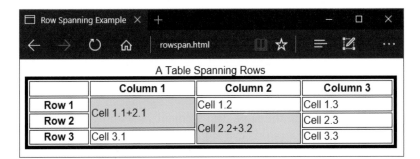

10 Reopen the HTML document once more, then insert an attribute into the table data element containing the text "Cell 1.3" and edit its content
`<td rowspan="3">Cell 1.3+2.3+3.3</td>`

Don't forget

Notice that by default, text in each cell is left-aligned and horizontally centered in merged cells.

11 Now, delete the table data elements containing the text "Cell 2.3" and "Cell 3.3" – as these cells are now spanned

12 Save the amended HTML document, then open it in your browser to see the cell spanning three rows in Column 3

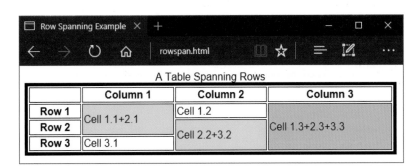

Spanning cells across columns

An individual table cell can be combined with others horizontally to span to the right across multiple columns of a table. The number of columns to be spanned is specified to a **colspan** attribute in the spanning cell's **<td>** tag. Cells in the columns being spanned must then be removed to maintain table symmetry.

HTML

colspan.html

1 Make a copy of the **table.html** document, created on pages 106-107, and rename it "colspan.html"

2 Change the document and table titles
<title>Column Spanning</title>
<caption>A Table Spanning Columns</caption>

3 In the table data element containing the text "Cell 1.1", insert an attribute in its opening tag and edit its content
<td colspan="2">Cell 1.1+1.2</td>

4 Now, delete the table data element containing the text "Cell 1.2" – as this cell is now spanned

{ }

CSS

table.css
(additions)

5 Save the HTML document, then re-open the **table.css** style sheet and add rules to style cells spanning columns
table#data td[colspan="2"] { background : aqua ; }
table#data td[colspan="3"] { background : yellow ; }

6 Save the style sheet, then open the web page in your browser to see the cell spanning two columns on Row 1

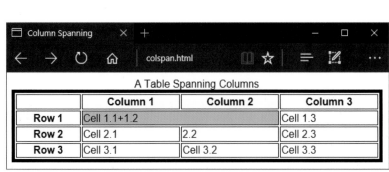

	Column 1	Column 2	Column 3
Row 1	Cell 1.1+1.2		Cell 1.3
Row 2	Cell 2.1	2.2	Cell 2.3
Row 3	Cell 3.1	Cell 3.2	Cell 3.3

A Table Spanning Columns

...cont'd

7 Reopen the HTML document, then insert an attribute into the table data element containing the text "Cell 2.1"
`<td colspan="3">Cell 2.1+2.2+2.3</td>`

8 Now, delete the table data elements containing the text "Cell 2.2" and "Cell 2.3" – as these cells are now spanned

9 Save the amended HTML document, then open it in your browser to see the cell spanning three columns on Row 2

Combined spans are rectangular – they cannot span an L-shape.

10 Reopen the HTML document once more, then insert another attribute into the table data element containing the text "Cell 2.1+2.2+2.3" and edit its content
`<td colspan="3" rowspan="2">`
`Cell 2.1+2.2+2.3+3.1+3.2+3.3</td>`

11 Now, delete the table data elements containing the text "Cell 3.1", "Cell 3.2" and "Cell 3.3" – cells now spanned

12 Save the amended HTML document, then open it in your browser to see the cell span three columns and two rows

Column spanning and row spanning can be combined to create large rectangular blocks of cells extending over multiple columns and across multiple rows.

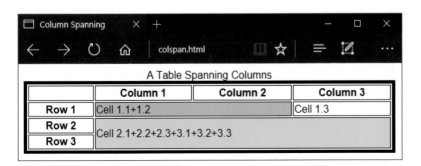

Adding a header and footer

Tables can be enhanced by the addition of special header and footer rows, above and below the regular table content, which provide additional table information.

In HTML5, table header information is contained between **<thead> </thead>** tags and table footer information is contained between **<tfoot> </tfoot>** tags. When a table has a **<thead>** and/or a **<tfoot>** element, all regular table rows must be enclosed between **<tbody> </tbody>** tags.

In long tables, rows can be grouped into separate table body sections using multiple **<tbody>** elements. When these are printed, each paper page can repeat the table header and footer information.

It is important to note that both the **<thead>** and **<tfoot>** elements must appear before the first **<tbody>** element within the **<table>** element, but after the **<caption>** element if one is present.

enhance.html

1 Make a copy of the **table.html** document, created on pages 106-107, and rename it "enhance.html"

2 Change the document and table titles
```
<title>Enhanced Table</title>
<caption>An Enhanced Table</caption>
```

3 Immediately after the caption, insert a table header containing a single row that spans all four columns
```
<thead>
<tr><td colspan="4">Header Information</tr>
</thead>
```

4 Immediately after the header, insert a table footer containing a single row that spans all four columns
```
<tfoot>
<tr><td colspan="4">Footer Information</tr>
</tfoot>
```

5 After the footer, add a table body element to enclose all the regular existing table rows
```
<tbody>
<!-- Existing row elements go here -->
</tbody>
```

6 After the table body element, insert a second table body element containing four more table rows

```
<tbody>
<tr><th colspan="4" class="next">Next section</tr>
<tr>
<th>Row 4<td>Cell 4.1<td>Cell 4.2<td>Cell 4.3</tr>
<tr>
<th>Row 5<td>Cell 5.1<td>Cell 5.2<td>Cell 5.3</tr>
<tr>
<th>Row 6<td>Cell 6.1<td>Cell 6.2<td>Cell 6.3</tr>
</tbody>
```

7 Save the HTML document, then reopen the **table.css** style sheet and add rules to style the table header, the second table body heading, and the table footer

```
table#data thead { background : aqua ; }
table#data th.next { background : yellow ; }
table#data tfoot { background : lime ; }
```

table.css
(additions)

8 Save the style sheet, then open the web page in your browser to see the enhanced table

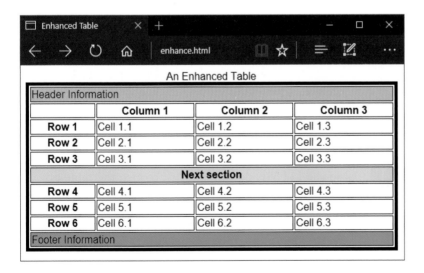

	Column 1	Column 2	Column 3
	An Enhanced Table		
Header Information			
	Column 1	Column 2	Column 3
Row 1	Cell 1.1	Cell 1.2	Cell 1.3
Row 2	Cell 2.1	Cell 2.2	Cell 2.3
Row 3	Cell 3.1	Cell 3.2	Cell 3.3
Next section			
Row 4	Cell 4.1	Cell 4.2	Cell 4.3
Row 5	Cell 5.1	Cell 5.2	Cell 5.3
Row 6	Cell 6.1	Cell 6.2	Cell 6.3
Footer Information			

Table headers and footers should only contain information – all table data should appear in the table body.

Aligning cell content

Typically, the default alignment of content in a **\<td>** table data cell is horizontally left-aligned and vertically centered, whereas content in a **\<th>** table heading cell is generally centered both horizontally and vertically. These defaults may be overridden by style rules, however, to align content horizontally and vertically.

A table cell's **text-align** property can specify values of **left**, **center** or **right** to align horizontally, and its **vertical-align** property can specify values of **top**, **middle** or **bottom** to align vertically.

Alignment rules may be specified for **\<tr>**, **\<tbody>**, **\<thead>** and **\<tfoot>** elements to control the horizontal and vertical content position in groups of cells. All **\<td>** and **\<th>** elements they contain automatically inherit the specified alignment values.

align.html

1 Make a copy of the **table.html** document, created on pages 106-107, and rename it "align.html"

2 Change the document and table titles
```
<title>Alignment Example</title>
<caption>A Table With Aligned Content</caption>
```

3 Now, edit each table row element to assign class names for styling content alignment
```
<tr class="default">
<th>Row 1<td>Cell 1.1<td>Cell 1.2<td>Cell 1.3</tr>
<tr class="center">
<th>Row 2<td>Cell 2.1<td>Cell 2.2<td>Cell 2.3</tr>
<tr class="bottom right">
<th>Row 3<td>Cell 3.1<td>Cell 3.2<td>Cell 3.3</tr>
```

table.css
(additions)

4 Save the HTML document, then reopen the **table.css** style sheet and add rules to style cell content alignment, cell height, and background color
```
table#data tr.default td
{ height : 30px ; background : yellow ;}
table#data tr.center td
{ text-align : center ; height : 30px; background : aqua ; }
table#data tr.right td
{ text-align : right ; height : 30px ; background : lime ; }
table#data tr.bottom  { vertical-align : bottom ; }
```

5 Save the style sheet, then open the web page in your browser to compare the cell content alignment on each row

A Table With Aligned Content

	Column 1	Column 2	Column 3
Row 1	Cell 1.1	Cell 1.2	Cell 1.3
Row 2	Cell 2.1	Cell 2.2	Cell 2.3
Row 3	Cell 3.1	Cell 3.2	Cell 3.3

Notice that the final row aligns content to the bottom of each cell in both **<th>** and **<td>** elements, as they inherit the rule applied to that row's **<tr>** element.

Table cells are automatically spaced apart at a fixed distance by default, but the cell spacing can be removed by a style rule specifying a **collapse** value to the table's **border-collapse** property. The outer table border can be explicitly suppressed by a style rule specifying a **none** value to the table's **border** property, and individual cell borders can be removed by a style rule specifying a value of **zero** to the cell's **border** property.

6 Edit the **align.html** document to assign class names for styling the table element and the top left empty table cell

```
<table id="data" class="no-border">
<tr><th class="cut-border">
<th>Column 1<th>Column 2<th>Column 3</tr>
```

Cell and table borders can be removed or styled individually using their **border-top**, **border-right**, **border-bottom**, and **border-left** properties.

7 Reopen the **table.css** style sheet again and add rules to remove the table and top left cell borders, and cell spacing

```
table#data.no-border
{ border-collapse : collapse ; border : none ; }
table#data tr th.cut-border { border : 0 ; }
```

8 Save the HTML document and style sheet once more, then reopen the web page to see the borders removed

A Table With Aligned Content

	Column 1	Column 2	Column 3
Row 1	Cell 1.1	Cell 1.2	Cell 1.3
Row 2	Cell 2.1	Cell 2.2	Cell 2.3
Row 3	Cell 3.1	Cell 3.2	Cell 3.3

It is particularly useful to remove the top left empty cell in tables without borders.

115

Grouping columns

Table columns that contain similar data can be virtually grouped together for styling purposes with **<colgroup> </colgroup>** tags. The opening **<colgroup>** tag can specify the number of columns to include in that group to a **span** attribute.

A **<table>** element can contain one or more **<colgroup>** elements to allow all the columns in a group to be styled alike, but have each group styled differently from other groups for contrast. These should appear at the start of the **<table>** element, immediately after the **<caption>** element, if one is present, but before **<thead>**, **<tfoot>**, **<tbody>** elements and table content.

When the **<colgroup>** element includes a **span** attribute, to specify how many columns to include in that group, the closing **</colgroup>** tag is required, but the element must remain empty – with nothing between the **<colgroup> </colgroup>** tags.

colgroup.html

1 Start with the HTML5 document type declaration
<!DOCTYPE HTML>

2 Add a root element containing head and body sections, with a link element pointing to a style sheet
<html lang="en">
<head>
<meta charset="UTF-8">
<title>Column Grouping</title>
<link rel="stylesheet" href="colgroup.css">
</head>
<body> <!-- Content to go here --> **</body>**
</html>

3 Within the body section, insert a table element that includes an identity for styling purposes
<table id="feb">
<!-- Table content to go here -->
</table>

4 Within the table element, first insert a table caption title
<caption>Monthly Calendar</caption>

5 Next, within the table element, insert elements grouping columns – with specified class names for styling each group
<colgroup span="5" class="weekday"></colgroup>
<colgroup span="2" class="weekend"></colgroup>

6 Now, within the table element, insert a table header and a table footer – each spanning seven columns

```
<thead>
<tr><th colspan="7">February 2021</tr>
</thead>

<tfoot> <tr><th colspan="7">Birthday</tr> </tfoot>
```

The table body in this example omits the optional **</td>** and **</tr>** closing tags to save page space, but including the **</tr>** tags more clearly denotes each row end.

7 Finally, in the table element, insert a table body containing seven columns, with one cell given an identity for styling

```
<tbody>
<tr><td>Mon<td>Tue<td>Wed<td>Thu
<td>Fri<td>Sat<td>Sun<tr><td>1<td>2<td>3<td>4
<td>5<td>6<td>7<tr><td>8<td>9<td>10<td>11
<td>12<td>13<td>14<tr><td>15<td>16<td>17
<td>18<td>19<td>20<td id="birthday">21<tr>
<td>22<td>23<td>24<td>25<td>26<td>27<td>28
</tbody>
```

8 Create a style sheet to color the column groups, remove cell spacing, and highlight the header, footer, and one cell

```
table#feb colgroup.weekday { background : aqua ; }
table#feb colgroup.weekend { background : yellow ; }

table#feb { width : 580px ; border-collapse : collapse ; }
table#feb  thead,tfoot { background : white ; color : red ; }
table#feb tbody { text-align : center ; }
table#feb tbody tr td#birthday { border : 2px solid red ; }
```

colgroup.css

9 Save the HTML document and style sheet, then open the web page in your browser to see how the column groups are clearly distinct from each other

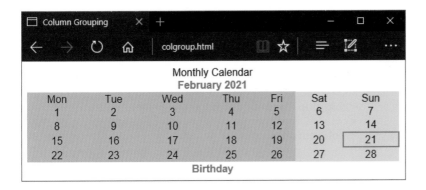

Setting column widths

Where a table simply has an overall width specified by a style rule, the browser will, by default, calculate the width of each column according to its content – columns with broad content will be wider than columns with slender content. Greater control over column width can be achieved using **<col>** tags to represent individual columns so rules can specify their size and appearance.

A single **<col>** element can also represent multiple columns by including a **span** attribute to specify a number of columns. So a style rule specifying a column width will be applied to all the columns that **<col>** element represents.

Optionally, **<col>** elements may be enclosed between **<colgroup> </colgroup>** tags to allow styling of both column groups and individual columns.

column.html

1 Start with the HTML5 document type declaration
<!DOCTYPE HTML>

2 Add a root element containing head and body sections, with a link element pointing to a style sheet
<html lang="en">
<head>
<meta charset="UTF-8">
<title>Column Styling</title>
<link rel="stylesheet" href="column.css">
</head>
<body> <!-- Content to go here --> **</body>**
</html>

3 Within the body section, insert a table element that includes an identity for styling purposes and a caption
<table id="jfk">
<caption>Breakfast Flights</caption>
<!-- Table content to go here -->
</table>

4 Next, in the table, insert a column group that includes a class name for styling and contains a single column
<colgroup class="sidebar">
<col>
</colgroup>

5 Now, insert two more column groups that include class names for both group styling and individual styling

```
<colgroup class="info">
<col class="stripe"> <col> <col class="stripe"></colgroup>
<colgroup class="info">
<col> <col class="stripe"> </colgroup>
```

6 After the column groups, insert a table header, a table footer, and a table body – each with six columns

```
<thead><tr><th colspan="6"><!-- Header --></thead>
<tfoot><tr><td colspan="6"><!-- Footer --></tfoot>
<tbody><!-- Rows with six cells each --></tbody>
```

7 Create a style sheet with rules to specify the appearance of the table, and its header, footer and data cells

```
table#jfk { width : 580px ; border-collapse : collapse ; }
table#jfk tbody th { background : blue ; color : white ; }
table#jfk tbody td { padding : 3px ; text-align : center ; }
table#jfk tfoot { font-size : small ; }
```

8 Next, add rules to specify the width of each column

```
table#jfk colgroup.sidebar col { width : 70px ; }
table#jfk colgroup.info col { width : 80px ; }
```

9 Now, add rules to style groups and individual columns

```
table#jfk colgroup.info { border-left : 2px solid white ; }
table#jfk colgroup col.stripe { background : aqua ; }
```

10 Save the HTML document and style sheet, then open the web page in your browser to see distinct column groups

The **•** character entity is used in this table footer to create bullet points.

column.css

119

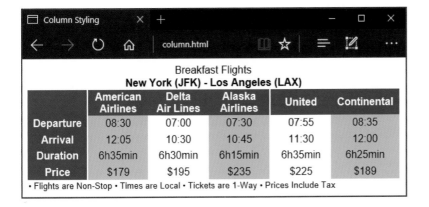

Breakfast Flights
New York (JFK) - Los Angeles (LAX)

	American Airlines	Delta Air Lines	Alaska Airlines	United	Continental
Departure	08:30	07:00	07:30	07:55	08:35
Arrival	12:05	10:30	10:45	11:30	12:00
Duration	6h35min	6h30min	6h15min	6h35min	6h25min
Price	$179	$195	$235	$225	$189

• Flights are Non-Stop • Times are Local • Tickets are 1-Way • Prices Include Tax

Notice how the styling separates the column groups.

Utilizing templates

HTML5 provides an interesting **<template>** element, which can be used to designate a group of elements that can be "cloned" by JavaScript. Typically, these elements will contain no data when designated as a template within the HTML document itself, but data can be dynamically inserted into the elements by a script. This feature is useful to dynamically populate lists or tables:

template.html

data.js

1 Start with the HTML5 document type declaration
<!DOCTYPE HTML>

2 Add a root element containing head and body sections, with two script elements and a link to a style sheet
```
<html lang="en">
<head>
<meta charset="UTF-8">
<title>Template Example</title>
<script src="data.js"></script>
<script src="template.js"></script>
<link rel="stylesheet" href="template.css">
</head>
<body>  <!-- Content to go here -->  </body>
</html>
```

3 Within the body section, insert a table that provides a template for its data row
```
<table>
<caption>High Performance Cars</caption>
<tr><th>Make<th>Model<th>BHP</tr>

<template id="row">
<tr><td><td><td></tr>
</template>

</table>
```

4 Save the HTML document, then create a script that defines an associative array of data keys and values
```
var data = [
{ "make":"Bugatti" , "model":"Veyron" , "bhp":"1200" } ,
{ "make":"Lambo" , "model":"Aventador" , "bhp":"740" } ,
{ "make":"Ferrari" , "model":"Berlinetta" , "bhp":"730" } ,
{ "make":"Chevrolet" , "model":"Camaro" , "bhp":"650" } ,
{ "make":"Pagani" , "model":"Zonda" , "bhp":"650" }
] ;
```

...cont'd

5 Save the data script, then create a functional script to write the data values into the template row

```
function init( )
{
  var template , i , car , clone , cells ;
  template = document.querySelector( "#row" ) ;
  for ( i = 0 ; i < data.length ; i++ )
  {
    car = data[ i ] ;
    clone = template.content.cloneNode( true ) ;
    cells = clone.querySelectorAll( "td" ) ;
    cells[ 0 ].textContent = car.make ;
    cells[ 1 ].textContent = car.model ;
    cells[ 2 ].textContent = car.bhp ;
    template.parentNode.appendChild( clone ) ;
  }
}
document.addEventListener("DOMContentLoaded", init, false) ;
```

template.js

6 Save the functional script, then create a style sheet with rules to specify the appearance of the table, and apply background color to alternate rows

```
table { font-family : sans-serif ; border : 1px solid black ; }
th                    { background : white ;  }
tr:nth-child( odd )   { background : coral ;  }
td                    { padding : 5px 50px ;  }
```

template.css

7 Save the style sheet, then open the HTML document in your web browser to see the table dynamically created

Beware

By default, the table's header row will also receive the alternating background color unless a rule specifies a background color for each **\<th\>** element.

Summary

- The HTML5 **<ul>** element creates an unordered bullet-point list that contains individual list items within **<li>** elements.

- A **list-style-type** property can specify that unordered list items should have a **disc, circle** or **square** bullet-point, or **none**.

- A **list-style-image** property can specify the URL of an image that should appear in place of list item bullet-points.

- The **<ol>** element creates an ordered numerical list that contains individual list items within **<li>** elements.

- A **list-style-type** property can specify how ordered list items should be numbered, such as **decimal, upper-latin**, or **none**.

- The **<dl>** element creates a definition list containing terms in **<dt>** elements and their descriptions in **<dd>** elements.

- The HTML5 **<table>** element creates a table, and may optionally first enclose a **<caption>** element to title the table.

- Each table row is created with a **<tr>** element to contain numerous **<th>** heading elements and **<td>** data elements.

- Table cells can span down other cells using the **rowspan** attribute, and cells to the right using the **colspan** attribute.

- Adding **<thead>** and **<tfoot>** elements, immediately after the **<caption>** element, enhances a table with a header and footer.

- Tables that have a header and footer must also enclose all regular table rows within a **<tbody>** element.

- A table cell's **text-align** and **vertical-align** properties can be used to specify its content's horizontal and vertical alignment.

- Table columns can be grouped using a **<colgroup>** element to specify the number of columns to group with its **span** attribute.

- Each table column can be represented by a **<col>** element so it can be individually styled.

- The **<template>** element can designate a group of elements that can be cloned to dynamically write lists and tables.

7

Embedding media content

This chapter demonstrates how to create content-rich web pages by embedding media objects within HTML5 documents.

124 Referencing figures

126 Selecting pictures

128 Embedding objects

130 Specifying parameters

132 Embedding in frames

134 Playing plugin movies

136 Embedding audio

138 Embedding video

140 Indicating progress

142 Summary

Referencing figures

With the latest HTML5 specifications, the web page author now has additional means by which to insert images into a web page. An **<img>** tag can be nested within a **<figure> </figure>** element to embed an image that is related to the main text content, but whose removal would not disrupt the text's meaning.

As the nested image, in effect, is now self-contained as a "figure", it can be positioned away from the text if desired, and referenced by a caption within a nested **<figcaption> </figcaption>** element:

figure.html

1 Start with the HTML5 document type declaration
<!DOCTYPE HTML>

2 Add a root element containing head and body sections, with a link element pointing to a style sheet
<html lang="en">
<head>
<meta charset="UTF-8">
<title>Figure Example</title>
<link rel="stylesheet" href="figure.css">
</head>
<body> <!-- Content to go here --> **</body>**
</html>

3 Within the body section, insert a heading
<h1>Web Development Stacks</h1>

4 Next, insert a captioned figure
<figure id="front-stack" >
<img src="front.png" alt="Front-end"
          width="118" height="108">
<figcaption>Figure 1:Front-end Technologies</figcaption>
</figure>

5 Now, insert text content that makes reference to the previous captioned figure
<p>Front-end development, also known as client-side development, is the practice of producing HTML documents, CSS style sheets, and JavaScript script code (Figure 1) for a website or Web Application - so a user can see and interact with them directly.</p>

Hot tip

Always refer to figures only by their label – avoid using reference terms like "in the figure on the right" so the document layout can be easily changed without creating confusion.

6 Insert a second captioned figure

```
<figure id="back-stack" >
<img src="back.png" alt="Back-end
        width="133" height="108" >
<figcaption>Figure 2:Back-end Technologies</figcaption>
</figure>
```

7 Now, insert text content that makes reference to the second captioned figure

```
<p>Back-end development, also known as server-side
development, is the practice of producing complex
websites using programming languages such as SQL, Java,
PHP or .NET (Figure 2) to provide features beyond front-
end capabilities.</p>
```

8 Create a style sheet to position each captioned figure and to specify some font styles

```
figure#front-stack { float : left ; margin-top : 0px ; }
figure#back-stack { float : right ; margin-top : 0px ; }
figcaption { font-size : smaller ; color : red ; }
p:first-letter { font-size : xx-large ; }
```

figure.css

9 Save the HTML document and style sheet, then open the web page in your browser to see the captioned figures

Web Development Stacks

Front-end development, also known as client-side development, is the practice of producing HTML documents, CSS style sheets, and JavaScript script code (Figure 1) for a website or Web Application - so a user can see and interact with them directly.

Figure 1:Front-end Technologies

Back-end development, also known as server-side development, is the practice of producing complex websites using programming languages such as SQL, Java, PHP or .NET (Figure 2) to provide features beyond front-end capabilities.

Figure 2:Back-end Technologies

Don't forget

You can discover more about back-end technologies with the companion books in this series on SQL, Java, PHP, and PHP & MySQL at www.ineasysteps.com

Selecting pictures

As web content is increasingly being accessed on small handheld devices, the latest HTML5 specifications allow the web page author to specify alternative images to be displayed on the web page according to the size of the device screen.

A **<picture> </picture>** element is used to contain multiple image sources from which the browser can select the most appropriate size. Each image source is specified to the **srcset** attribute of a nested **<source>** element, and the minimum screen width suitable for that image is specified to its **media** attribute. The assignment requires an unusual syntax that states the size to a **min-width** property within **( )** parentheses. For example, to specify that an image is suitable for display only on devices whose screen width exceeds 500 pixels with **media="(min-width : 500px)"**.

Usefully, the **<picture> </picture>** element can enclose a final regular **<img>** element to specify the image to be displayed on older web browsers that do not support this selection feature:

The **<picture>** tag, and the ability for it to contain multiple **<source>** elements for responsive image selection, is a great new feature introduced in the HTML 5.1 specifications.

picture.html

1 Start with the HTML5 document type declaration
<!DOCTYPE HTML>

2 Add a root element containing head and body sections
<html lang="en">
<head>
<meta charset="UTF-8">
<title>Picture Example</title>
</head>
<body> <!-- Content to go here --> </body>
</html>

3 Within the body section, insert a container element
<picture>

<!-- Image sources to be inserted here -->

</picture>

4 Next, insert an image source for display only on devices whose screen width exceeds 500 pixels
<source media="(min-width : 500px)" srcset="large.png" >

The **<source>** element does not require a closing tag. It is also used within the **<audio>** element, described on page 136, and with the **<video>** element, described on page 138.

5 Now, insert an image source for display only on smaller devices whose screen width exceeds 200 pixels
<source media="(min-width : 200px)" srcset="small.png" >

6 Finally, insert an image source for display only on older browsers that do not support the selection feature
**<img alt="Regular Guy" src="medium.png"
        width="103" height="125">**

large.png – 205 x 250
medium.png – 103 x 125
small.png – 62 x 75

7 Save the HTML document, then open the web page full-screen in a desktop web browser to see the large image

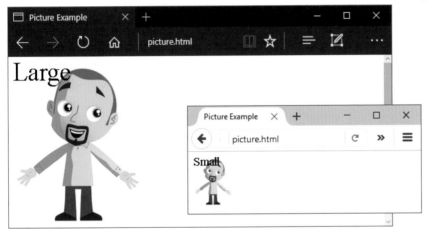

8 Open the web page on a small device, or re-size the browser window, to see the small image

9 Open the page on an old browser to see the medium image

Hot tip

If you examine the browser cache you should see that it has only efficiently downloaded the appropriate image to be displayed, not all images.

Embedding objects

An external resource can be embedded into an HTML5 document using **<object> </object>** tags to define the resource. When the resource is an image it will be treated much like those specified by **<img>** elements, otherwise a plugin may be sought to process the resource. The **<object>** element can specify the resource's URL to its **data** attribute and the resource type to its **type** attribute. The resource type must be a valid MIME type describing the resource.

This table lists some popular MIME types. Further details can be found on the W3C website at www.w3.org

MIME Type:	Object File Format:
image/png	PNG image resource
image/jpeg	JPG, JPEG, JPE image resource
image/gif	GIF image resource
image/svg+xml	SVG vector image resource
text/plain	TXT regular plain text resource
text/html	HTM, HTML markup text resource
application/pdf	PDF portable document resource
application/msword	DOC Word document resource
application/x-java-applet	CLASS Java applet resource
audio/x-wav	WAV sound resource
audio/mpeg	MP3 music resource
video/mp4	MP4 video resource
video/x-mpeg	MPEG, MPG, MPE video resource
video/x-msvideo	AVI video resource
video/x-msv-wmv	WMV Windows video resource
video/quicktime	MOV QuickTime video resource

Beware

All **<object>** elements must contain at least one **data** attribute or one **type** attribute.

Each **<object>** element can specify dimensions in which to display visual content using its **width** and **height** attributes. Where the resource is an image, the **<object>** element can also include a **usemap** attribute to specify the name of an image map, just like those produced for an **<img>** element.

Optionally, fallback text can be included between the **<object> </object>** tags that will only be displayed by the browser in the event that the resource cannot be embedded within the document. For example, when an appropriate plugin cannot be found.

...cont'd

1 Start with the HTML5 document type declaration
`<!DOCTYPE HTML>`

pdf.html

2 Add a root element containing head and body sections
```
<html lang="en">
<head>
<meta charset="UTF-8">
<title>Embedding Objects</title>
</head>
<body> <!-- Content to go here --> </body>
</html>
```

3 Within the body section, insert a paragraph wrapper
```
<p>This is text in the main document that...<br>
<!-- Resource to be embedded here -->
<br>...continues around an embedded resource.</p>
```

4 Within the paragraph, insert a PDF object to embed
```
<object data="piechart.pdf" type="application/pdf"
        width="580" height="310">
[ PDF Document - May require the Adobe Reader plugin ]
</object>
```

piechart.pdf
(external resource)

5 Save the HTML document alongside the specified resource file, then open the web page to see it embedded

129

Hot tip

If you can disable PDF support then re-open this example. You will see the fallback text appear in place of the embedded PDF document.

Java applets can pose a security threat, so trusted websites need to be added to the Exception Site List under Web Settings in the Java Control Panel in order to run their applets.

Specifying parameters

Some external resources embedded into an HTML5 document can be passed "parameter" values to the plugin processing that resource to control its execution. For example, a plugin's "autoplay" property might be passed a "false" value to suppress automatic playback when the resource gets embedded into the web page.

An appropriate plugin will be sought after the resource type is identified by the MIME type specified to an **<object>** element's **type** attribute. Parameter values for that particular plugin can then be specified using **<param>** elements nested between the **<object> </object>** tags. Each **<param>** element must have both a **name** attribute and a **value** attribute, which pass the parameters to the plugin as a name/value pair. For example, automatic playback might be suppressed with this element:

<param name="autoplay" value="false">

The permissible parameter names and values are specific to each object, but are given in their documentation. For example, the permissible parameter names and values for Java applets are provided in each applet's documentation – as they have been specified by the applet creator to suit that particular application. In this case, the Java Runtime Environment (JRE) uses the parameters specified in each **<param>** element to control execution of the applet.

1 Start with the HTML5 document type declaration
<!DOCTYPE HTML>

2 Add a root element containing head and body sections
<html lang="en">
<head>
<meta charset="UTF-8">
<title>Embedding Applet Example</title>
</head>
<body> <!-- Content to go here --> **</body>**
</html>

3 Within the body section, insert a paragraph wrapper
**<p>This is text in the main document that...
**
<!-- Resource to be embedded here -->
**
...continues around an embedded resource.</p>**

applet.html

Java applet parameters are specific to each applet, and are given in the documentation that accompanies the applet.

4 Within the paragraph, insert an applet object to embed

```
<object type="application/x-java-applet"
                width="580" height="300">
[ Java Applet - Requires Java Runtime Environment (JRE) ]
</object>
```

5 Before the fallback text within the object element, insert a parameter specifying the applet resource's URL

```
<param name="code" value="barchart.class">
```

6 Next, within the object element, insert parameters defining data to be used by this particular applet

```
<param name="title" value="Web Browser Popularity">
<param name="val_1" value="23">
<param name="description_1" value="Internet Explorer">
<param name="val_2" value="11">
<param name="description_2" value="Firefox">
<param name="val_3" value="55">
<param name="description_3" value="Google Chrome">
<param name="val_4" value="4">
<param name="description_4" value="Safari">
<param name="val_5" value="6">
<param name="description_5" value="Microsoft Edge">
```

7 Save the HTML document alongside the specified resource file, then open the web page to see it embedded

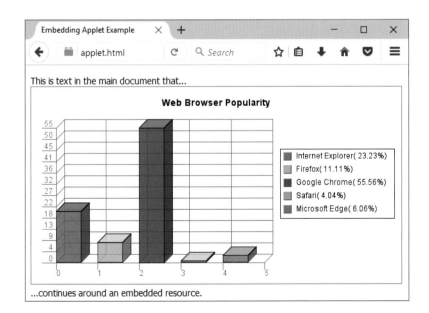

This is text in the main document that...

Web Browser Popularity

Internet Explorer(23.23%)
Firefox(11.11%)
Google Chrome(55.56%)
Safari(4.04%)
Microsoft Edge(6.06%)

...continues around an embedded resource.

barchart.class
(external resource)

This particular Java applet also lets you specify custom colors and legend details. These are unlisted here due to the limitations of page space.

If fallback text is included, it should appear just before the closing **</object>** tag.

Embedding in frames

External resources can be embedded in an HTML5 document within an "inline frame" using **<iframe> </iframe>** tags. These create a fixed area on the page in which to display the embedded resource. The inline frame's dimensions must be specified to the **<iframe>** element's **width** and **height** attributes, and the URL of the external resource to its **src** attribute. Where the dimensions of the external resource exceed those of the inline frame, the browser automatically adds scroll bars so the user can view the entire content.

Each **<iframe>** element may also optionally contain a **name** attribute to specify a unique identifier for that frame. This allows hyperlinks to then load the URL specified to their **href** attribute into the inline frame (rather than replace the entire page) by assigning the frame name to a **target** attribute in the **<a>** element. For example, a hyperlink could target an inline frame named "topbox" with **<a href="some.html" target="topbox">**.

Typically, inline frames are useful to provide supplemental content while maintaining a compact page format.

iframe.html

A fallback message can be provided between the **<iframe> </iframe>** tags to be displayed when inline frame support is disabled.

1 Start with the HTML5 document type declaration
<!DOCTYPE HTML>

2 Add a root element containing head and body sections, with a link element pointing to a style sheet
<html lang="en">
<head>
<meta charset="UTF-8">
<title>Inline Frame Example</title>
<link rel="stylesheet" href="iframe.css">
</head>
<body> <!-- Content to go here --> **</body>**
</html>

3 Within the body section, insert an article containing a heading and descriptive paragraph, and with a specified class name for positional styling purposes
<article class="left220">
<h3>Concept Cars</h3>
<p>Many of the creative and innovative concept cars premiered at the recent motor show left the audience in eager anticipation of their production.</p>
</article>

4 Next, in the body, as an aside, insert an inline frame to load a document containing relevant text and illustrative photographs positioned horizontally side-by-side

```
<aside>
<iframe src="concept.html" width="300" height="200">
[ Framed Document - Requires Iframe Support ]
</iframe>
</aside>
```

concept.html
(external resource)

5 Now, create a style sheet to size the article and position it to the left of the inline frame

```
article.left220
{ width : 220px ; float : left ; margin-right : 20px ; }
```

iframe.css

6 Save the HTML document and style sheet then open the web page to see the article and the inline frame content

133

Hot tip

Drag the scrollbar to see the images. Embedding documents within inline frames is particularly favored on property websites to accompany property descriptions with photographs in a compact page format.

Embedding plugin movies

The **<object>** and **<iframe>** elements, described in the previous examples on pages 128-133, can be used to embed other documents into a web page. External resources that provide interactive content, such as Flash "movies", can more easily be embedded by an **<embed>** element.

Each **<embed>** tag should specify the URL of the external interactive resource to its **src** attribute. For a Flash movie, this will be the location of the ShockWave Flash (SWF) file. In order for the browser to seek an appropriate plugin, the movie's MIME type should also be specified to its **type** attribute. For a Flash movie, this will be "application/x-shockwave-flash". Additionally, the dimensions of the area in which to display the movie on the page are specified to **width** and **height** attributes.

Web browsers that support HTML5 also support Scalable Vector Graphics (SVG). Unlike bitmap graphic formats such as PNG, which store their graphic information as the color of each pixel, vector graphics store the graphic information as a series of "paths". This is a highly efficient way to describe graphics. Most importantly, vector graphics can be scaled without loss of fidelity. This means that they can be infinitely enlarged without suffering the pixelation experienced when enlarging bitmap images.

SVG Vector x3   PNG Bitmap x3

SVG is not actually part of HTML5, but is a specification based on the eXtensible Markup Language (XML), so it describes vector images in text files. These can be created manually, but it's far simpler to use a vector graphics editor such as Adobe Illustrator.

Just as Flash movies incorporate ActionScript for functionality, SVG can incorporate JavaScript to create interactive SVG movies. These can be embedded in HTML5 by specifying the MIME type "image/svg+xml" to the **<embed>** element's **type** attribute.

Beware

Support for browser plugins, such as Adobe Flash Player, is slowly disappearing, as HTML5 provides better and more secure alternatives.

Hot tip

Static SVG images can be embedded using the **<img>** element – just like any other image.

1 Start a new HTML5 document
```
<!DOCTYPE HTML>
<html lang="en">
<head> <meta charset="UTF-8">
<title>Embedding Movies</title>
</head>
<body> <!-- Content to go here --> </body>
</html>
```

movie.html

2 In the body section, insert elements to embed two movies
```
<embed src="movie.swf" width="270" height="202"
            type="application/x-shockwave-flash" >
<embed src="movie.svg" width="283" height="202"
            type="image/svg+xml" >
```

movie.swf   movie.svg
(external resources)

3 Save the HTML document, then open the web page in your browser to see the embedded movies and select colors to interact with the movies

Don't forget

You can examine how JavaScript has been incorporated into this SVG document by downloading the examples archive from www.ineasysteps. com/resource-centre/ downloads/

Embedding audio

External audio resources, such as MP3 music files, can be embedded in an HTML5 document using **<audio> </audio>** tags.

The **<audio>** element can include an **src** attribute, to specify the URL of the audio resource to embed, and may include additional attributes to determine how the audio resource will be used:

● **autoplay** – a Boolean attribute that specifies the browser should immediately begin playing the audio resource.

● **loop** – a Boolean attribute that specifies the browser should play the audio resource repeatedly.

● **controls** – a Boolean attribute that specifies the browser should display user controls to start or stop the audio playing.

● **preload** – accepts values of "auto" or "none" to suggest the browser should load the audio resource so it is ready to play.

Boolean attributes, like the **autoplay**, **loop** and **controls** attributes, need have no assigned value – their presence alone within the element is sufficient for the browser to understand their purpose.

Browsers rely upon an in-built "codec" (**co**der-**dec**oder) to decode audio resources so they can be played. Sadly, not all browsers incorporate the same audio codec:

● **Advanced Audio Coding (AAC)** – codec "mp4a.40.2" is supported by modern browsers such as Microsoft Edge, Internet Explorer, Firefox, and Chrome for MP3 audio.

● **Ogg audio** – codec "vorbis" is supported by other browsers for audio files in OGG format.

This inconsistency therefore requires audio resources to be encoded twice for playback across all browsers. Two **<source>** elements may be nested within an **<audio>** element for this purpose, rather than specifying a single resource URL to an **src** attribute in the **<audio>** tag. For each file format, the **<source>** elements can then specify their resource URL to an **src** attribute, and their MIME type to a **type** attribute. The browser will only load the supported audio resource for playback.

1 Start a new HTML5 document

```
<!DOCTYPE HTML>
<html lang="en">
<head> <meta charset="UTF-8">
<title>Audio Example</title>
</head>
<body> <!-- Content to go here --> </body>
</html>
```

audio.html

2 In the body section, insert an element to embed an audio resource in the MP3 format for automatic playback

```
<audio src="audio.mp3" autoplay > [ Fallback ] </audio>
```

audio.mp3   audio.ogg
(external resources)

3 Save the HTML document, then open the web page to hear automatic audio playback in supported browsers

4 Next, replace both previous attributes with one to display user controls for audio playback

```
<audio controls> <!-- Sources to go here --> </audio>
```

5 Now, in the audio element, insert elements to specify audio resources to be embedded for all browsers

```
<source src="audio.mp3" type="audio/mpeg" >
<source src="audio.ogg" type="audio/ogg" >
```

Avoid automatic audio playback on websites, as some users detest the autoplay feature.

6 Save the HTML document again, then open the web page in any browser and use the controls to hear playback

137

Embedding video

W3C®

You can discover more about the WebVTT subtitle format online at www.w3.org/TR/webvtt1

138

Hot tip

The Advanced Video Coding standard is also often referred to by its project name of "H.264".

VTT

video.vtt

External video resources, such as MP4 video files, can be embedded in an HTML5 document using **<video> </video>** tags.

To determine how the video resource will be used, the **<video>** element can include **src**, **autoplay**, **loop**, **controls** and **preload** attributes, just like the **<audio>** element in the previous example. Additionally, the dimensions of the area in which to display the video on the page can be specified to **width** and **height** attributes.

As with audio resources, browsers rely upon an in-built "codec" (**co**der-**dec**oder) to decode video resources so they can be played. Sadly, not all browsers incorporate the same video codec:

- **Advanced Video Coding (AVC)** – codec "avc1.42E01E" is supported by modern browsers such as Microsoft Edge, Internet Explorer, Firefox, and Chrome for MP4 video

- **Ogg video** – codec "theora" is supported by other browsers for video files in OGV format

This inconsistency requires video resources to be encoded twice for playback across all browsers, and embedded using two **<source>** elements nested within a **<video>** element. For each file format, the **<source>** elements can then specify their resource URL to an **src** attribute, and the MIME type of each video file can be specified to the **type** attribute. The browser will only load the supported video resource for playback.

A **<track>** tag may also be nested within a **<video>** element to specify the location of a Web Video Text Tracks (WebVTT) subtitles file to its **src** attribute. The tag must also include a Boolean **default** attribute to use the specified file. The subtitles file must be in a very specific format that begins with "WEBVTT". Start and end timing cues are added on new lines in the format "HH:MM:SS:sss" and separated by " --> ". The associated subtitle caption appears on a new line below each timing cue, like this:

WEBVTT

00:00:01:000 --> 00:00:04:000
Playing video with "HTML5 in easy steps"

00:00:05:000 --> 00:00:06:000
Thanks for watching.

1 Start a new HTML5 document

```
<!DOCTYPE HTML>
<html lang="en">
<head> <meta charset="UTF-8">
<title>Video Example</title>
</head>
<body> <!-- Content to go here --> </body>
</html>
```

video.html

2 In the body section, insert an element to embed a video resource and display user controls for video playback

```
<video controls >
<!-- Sources to go here -->
[ Fallback ]
</video>
```

3 Next, in the video element, insert elements to embed a video and specify a subtitle file

```
<source src="video.ogv" type="video/ogg" >
<source src="video.mp4" type="video/mp4" >
<track src="video.vtt" default>
```

video.mp4   video.ogv
(external resources)

4 Save the HTML document, then open the web page in any browser and use the controls to see video playback

Don't forget

This short video displays the first subtitle for 4 seconds, and displays the second subtitle at the end of playback.

The **<progress>** tag is a new element introduced in HTML 5.1.

Indicating progress

If you prefer not to provide the browser's standard controls for playback of audio or video, the **controls** attribute can be omitted from the **<audio>** and **<video>** tags. The JavaScript **play()** and **pause()** methods of an embedded media object can then be called to control playback from an **onclick** event-handler script function.

A visual indicator of media playback can be displayed using a **<progress> </progress>** element to present a "progress bar". Within the **<progress>** tag, a **value** attribute determines the extent of progress towards completion. This can be dynamically updated in synchronization with media playback from an **ontimeupdate** event-handler script function.

Embedded media objects have a **currentTime** property, which stores the elapsed time since playback began, and a **duration** property that stores total playback time. These can be used to calculate playback progress as a percentage:

progress.html

1 Start a new HTML5 document that incorporates a script
```
<!DOCTYPE HTML>
<html lang="en">
<head> <meta charset="UTF-8">
<title>Progress Example</title>
<script src="progress.js"></script>
</head>
<body> <!-- Content to go here --> </body>
</html>
```

Include an **id** attribute in the **<audio>** tag to reference the media from script, and in all other tags that the script needs to reference.

2 In the body section, insert elements to embed an audio resource for manual playback
```
<audio id="snd">
<source src="audio.mp3" type="audio/mpeg" >
<source src="audio.ogg" type="audio/ogg" > [ Fallback ]
</audio>
```

3 Next, insert an image button to control payback
```
<img id="ctl" src="ctl.png" width="32"
                    height="32" alt="Control" >
```

4 Now, insert elements to present a visual indicator and calculated percentage as playback proceeds
```
<progress id="bar" value="0"></progress>
<span id="num">[Audio]</span>
```

...cont'd

5 Begin a script with a function to initialize variables when the HTML document has loaded

```
function init()
{
  var run = true ;
  var snd = document.getElementById( "snd" ) ;
  var ctl = document.getElementById( "ctl" ) ;
  var bar = document.getElementById( "bar" ) ;
  var num = document.getElmentById( "num" ) ;

  /* Event-handler functions go here */
}
onload = init ;
```

progress.js

6 Insert a function to control playback

```
ctl.onclick = function() {
  ( run ) ? snd.play() : snd.pause() ;
  run = !run ; }
```

The control will play or pause playback according to the Boolean value of the **run** variable.

7 Insert a function to display playback progress

```
snd.ontimeupdate = function() {
  bar.value = ( snd.currentTime / snd.duration );
  num.innerHTML = Math.floor(100 * bar.value) + "%"; }
```

8 Save the HTML document and script file, then open the web page in a browser and click the button to see playback progress

The **currentTime** and **duration** properties store time in seconds as floating-point values, so need to be rounded down with **Math.floor()**.

Summary

- The **<figure>** and **<figcaption>** tags can be used to embed a captioned reference image within an HTML document.

- A **<picture>** element can contain several **<source>** tags to provide a variety of image sizes for different screen widths.

- The **<object>** **</object>** tags can be used to embed external resources within an HTML document.

- An **<object>** tag can specify the size of a display area, the URL of an external resource, and the resource's MIME type.

- Multiple **<param>** elements can be nested within an **<object>** element to specify parameters to **name** and **value** attributes.

- External resources can be embedded into an inline frame with an **<iframe>** element that specifies the size of a display area, and a **name** attribute so it can become the target of a hyperlink.

- Each **<object>** and **<iframe>** element can include fallback text to be displayed when the resource cannot be embedded.

- External resources can be embedded into an HTML document using **<embed>** tags.

- An **<embed>** tag can specify the size of a display area, the URL of an external resource, and the resource's MIME type.

- External audio resources can be embedded into an HTML document using **<audio>** **</audio>** tags, and external video resources can be embedded using **<video>** **</video>** tags.

- Each **<audio>** and **<video>** element should include nested **<source>** elements to specify the resource URL to their **src** attribute, and its MIME type to their **type** attribute.

- A **<video>** element can contain a nested **<track>** element to specify a subtitle file in the WebVTT format.

- The **<progress>** element can be used to provide a visual indicator of media playback.

8 Building input forms

This chapter demonstrates **144** Submitting forms

how to build web forms **146** Gathering text input

within HTML5 documents **148** Controlling input type

for the submission of **150** Providing text areas

data to a web server. **152** Checking boxes

154 Choosing radio buttons

156 Selecting options

158 Utilizing hidden data

160 Pushing buttons

162 Using images for submission

164 Adding logos to buttons

166 Labeling form controls

168 Listing data options

170 Uploading files

172 Summary

Submitting forms

Web page forms are built from a number of HTML5 component elements that submit data to a web server for processing. Each of these elements include a **name** attribute and a **value** attribute so the data assigned to these attributes can be processed by the associated name=value pairs. For example, where an element's **name** attribute is assigned "Brand" and its **value** attribute is assigned "Ford" the name=value pair represents the data as Brand=Ford.

All form components are enclosed between **<form>** **</form>** tags. Each opening **<form>** tag should include a **method** attribute, specifying which HTTP method is to be used to submit the form, and an **action** attribute specifying the URL of a web server script that is to be used to process the submitted data.

The **method** attribute can be assigned values of "GET" or "POST". Submission via the preferred GET method appends the data to the URL, whereas submission via the POST method encodes the data differently and can be used when the GET method fails.

Typically, an HTML form will have a "Submit" button that the user clicks to submit data for processing. This is created by assigning the value "submit" to a **type** attribute of an **<input>** tag. Additionally, this tag may include **name** and **value** attributes to submit data assigned to them as a name=value pair.

In order to demonstrate form submission and web server response, the examples throughout this chapter use a personal web server. This emulates submission of data to an external web server but is installed locally on the host computer. Like many web servers, it has a directory named "htdocs" in which to deposit web pages and can be addressed by the domain name "localhost", or alternatively by the IP address "127.0.0.1". For example, to view the default web page entitled "index.html" with the server running, you can enter **http://localhost/index.html** in the browser address field, or alternatively enter **http://127.0.0.1/index.html**

To provide a response from the web server, the **htdocs** directory contains a custom server-side script named "echo.pl" that echos the submitted name=value data in an HTML response document – in each example, its URL is assigned to the form's **action** attribute. The web server's response simply displays the submitted values in a table to confirm the form data was received.

The examples in this chapter use the free Abyss Personal Edition web server available from **aprelium.com**

The server-side scripts used to process the examples in this chapter are written in the Perl language and require the installation of ActivePerl support on Windows systems. The free ActivePerl Community Edition can be downloaded from **activestate.com/ activeperl/downloads**

① Start a new HTML5 document
```
<!DOCTYPE HTML>
<html lang="en">
<head>
<meta charset="UTF-8">
<title>Form Submission</title>
</head>
<body> <!-- Content to go here --> </body>
</html>
```

submit.html

② In the body section, insert an element to submit form data to a server-side script using the GET method
```
<form method="GET" action="http://localhost/echo.pl" >
<!-- Form components to go here -->
</form>
```

③ Now, in the form element, insert a paragraph containing a submission button – whose value will appear on the button
```
<p>
<input type="submit"
        name="My Submit Button Name"
        value="My Submit Button Value">
</p>
```

To process the examples in this chapter, the files **echo.pl**, **echo.css**, **perl.png** and **abyss.png** should be placed in the "htdocs" directory of a local running web server – these are located in the download archive for this book available from **ineasysteps.com/ resource-centre/ downloads**

145

④ Save the HTML document, then open the web page in your browser and click the button to submit the data assigned to its name=value pair, and to see the response

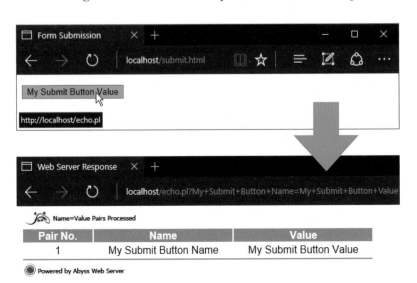

Notice the data appended in the browser's address field by the GET method – you can submit via the POST method to prevent this for sensitive data.

Gathering text input

An HTML5 form can provide text boxes where the user can input data for submission to the web server for processing. These are created by assigning the value "text" to the **type** attribute of an **<input>** tag, and a name to its **name** attribute. Upon submission, the data in the text box is sent as the value associated with the text box name as a name=value pair. Optionally, the **<input>** tag can include a **value** attribute to specify a default value. A text box for the input of a password is created by assigning the value "password" to the **type** attribute of an **<input>** tag. This functions just like any other text box, except it does not display its contents as readable text. Both text and password **<input>** elements can optionally include other attributes to control their performance:

- **size** – the width of the text box in average character widths
- **minlength** and **maxlength** – permissible number of characters
- **min** and **max** – permissible range of numeric values
- **placeholder** – provides a data entry hint to the user
- **readonly** – the default value in the text box cannot be changed
- **disabled** – the text box is grayed out and will not be submitted

text.html

1 Start a new HTML5 document
```
<!DOCTYPE HTML>
<html lang="en">
<head>
<meta charset="UTF-8">
<title>Text Input Example</title>
</head>
<body> <!-- Content to go here --> </body>
</html>
```

2 In the body section, insert a form element containing a submit button to send form data by the GET method
```
<form method="GET" action="http://localhost/echo.pl" >
<!-- Text input elements to go here -->
<p><input type="submit" value="Submit Form"></p>
</form>
```

3 Now, in the form element, insert a definition list element
```
<dl>
<!-- Terms and descriptions to go here -->
</dl>
```

...cont'd

In the definition list, insert terms and descriptions

```
<dt>User Name :
<dd><input type="text" name="Name">
<dt>Password :
<dd><input type="password" name="Password">
<dt>City :
<dd><input type="text" name="City" value="Dallas">
<dt>Area :
<dd><input type="text" name="Area"
                    value="Downtown" disabled>
<dt>State :
<dd><input type="text" name="State"
                    value="Texas" readonly >
<dt>Zip Code :
<dd><input type="text" name="Zip Code"
                    size="5" maxlength="5">
```

Save the HTML document, then open the web page in your browser, enter some data and submit the form

Notice that the **readonly** attribute ensures that the State cannot be edited, the **maxlength** attribute limits the Zip Code to 5 characters in length, and the **disabled** attribute grays out the Area text box – so that element will not be submitted to the server for processing.

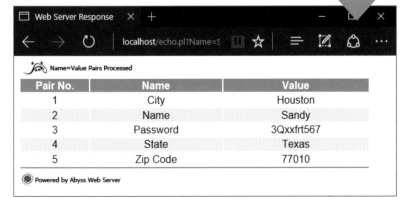

Pair No.	Name	Value
1	City	Houston
2	Name	Sandy
3	Password	3Qxxfrt567
4	State	Texas
5	Zip Code	77010

The server-side script echos the name=value pairs arranged in alphabetical name order, irrespective of their order on the page.

Controlling input type

An HTML5 form **<input>** tag can enforce its completion by including the **required** keyword. It can also control what the user is permitted to submit by the value assigned to its **type** attribute. Many of the input types listed in the table below prohibit submission of the form if the user enters a value that is not permitted, and issue an error notice. Some also provide special controls that allow the user to easily select a permitted value.

The **month**, **week**, and **datetime-local** input types are new types introduced in HTML 5.1.

Type:	Permitted input:
text	String of text
password	String of text (obscured by browser)
url	Valid URL protocol and domain address
email	Valid email address
date	Date in mm/dd/yyyy format
month	Month and year
week	Week number and year
time	Time in HH:MM format
datetime-local	Date and time as mm-dd-yy HH:MM
number	Numeric integer value
range	Numeric integer value (slider)
color	Color in #RRGGBB hexadecimal format
file	File path address (browse)

type.html

1 Start a new HTML5 document

```
<!DOCTYPE HTML>
<html lang="en">
<head>
<meta charset="UTF-8">
<title>Input Types Example</title>
</head>
<body> <!-- Content to go here --> </body>
</html>
```

2 In the body section, insert a form element containing a submit button to send form data by the GET method

```
<form method="GET" action="http://localhost/echo.pl" >
<!-- Input elements to go here -->
<p><input type="submit" value="Submit Form"></p>
</form>
```

3 Now, in the form element, insert a paragraph containing four controlling input elements

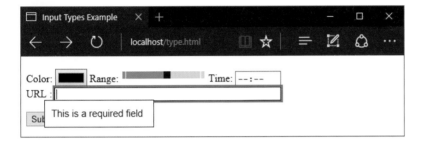

```
<p>Color: <input type="color" name="color">Range:
<input type="range" name="range" min="1" max="10">
Time: <input type="time" name="time"> <br>URL :
<input type="url" name="url" size="54" required ></p>
```

4 Save the HTML document, then try to submit the form

5 Enter a valid URL and enter permitted values, using special controls for other inputs, then submit the form

Color Picker

Range Picker

Time Picker

Pair No.	Name	Value
1	color	#40bfbf
2	range	8
3	time	11:30
4	url	http://www.ineasysteps.com

Providing text areas

An HTML5 form can provide a multi-line text field where the user can input data for submission to the web server for processing. These are created by **<textarea> </textarea>** tags that may enclose default text content. The **<textarea>** tag should include a **name** attribute that will be associated with the element's content upon submission as a name=value pair. Additionally, this tag must include a **rows** attribute, to specify the number of visible text lines, and a **cols** attribute to specify the field width in average character widths. Optionally, it may also include a **readonly** attribute to prevent the user editing its content.

When submitting large bodies of text, you must be aware of some limitations of the GET method. This varies by browser, but Internet Explorer typically allows the URL to append up to around 200 characters. The POST method provides much larger capacity, as the text is sent as "Form Data" along with the HTTP header, not simply appended to the URL:

Don't forget

Unlike a text **<input>** element, the **<textarea>** element has no **value** attribute – as its content is treated as its value.

textarea.html

1 Start a new HTML5 document
```
<!DOCTYPE HTML>
<html lang="en">
<head>
<meta charset="UTF-8">
<title>Text Area Example</title>
</head>
<body> <!-- Content to go here --> </body>
</html>
```

2 In the body section, insert a form element containing a submit button to send form data by the POST method
```
<form method="POST" action="http://localhost/echo.pl" >
<!-- Text area element to go here -->
<p><input type="submit" value="Submit Form"></p>
</form>
```

3 Now, in the form element, insert a text input area that has 8 rows and is 70 average character widths wide
```
<textarea name="The Future Web"
                    rows="8" cols="70">

</textarea>
```

4 Save the HTML document, then open the web page in your browser, enter some data and submit the form

...cont'd

Beware

The average character width may vary between browsers – so the physical size of the text area field may vary too.

5 The text is not appended to the URL, so examine the response headers to see it has been sent as "Form Data"

Hot tip

You can use the Developer Tools in the Google Chrome web browser to examine response headers – as illustrated here.

Checking boxes

An HTML5 form can provide a visual checkbox "on/off" switch that the user can toggle to include or exclude its associated data for submission to the server. When the box is checked, the switch is set to "on" and its name=value pair will be submitted, but when the box is unchecked, the switch is set to "off" and its name=value pair is not submitted. A checkbox is created by assigning the value "checkbox" to the **type** attribute of an **<input>** tag. This tag must also include a **name** attribute and a **value** attribute to specify the name=value pair values. Optionally, this tag may also include a Boolean **checked** attribute to set the initial state of the switch to "on" – so a check mark will automatically appear in the checkbox. Checkbox names may be individually unique, or several checkboxes can share a common name to allow the user to select multiple values for the same named property. In this case, the selected values are returned by the server as a comma-separated list where name=value,value,value. Multiple checkboxes that share a common name can be visually grouped by surrounding their **<input>** elements by **<fieldset>** **</fieldset>** tags. These may also contain **<legend>** **</legend>** tags to state a common group name:

The **<fieldset>** element only groups the related elements it encloses for visual presentation – it does not associate them programmatically.

checkbox.html

1 Start a new HTML5 document
```
<!DOCTYPE HTML>
<html lang="en">
<head>
<meta charset="UTF-8">
<title>Checkbox Example</title>
</head>
<body> <!-- Content to go here --> </body>
</html>
```

2 In the body section, insert a form element containing a submit button to send form data by the GET method
```
<form method="GET" action="http://localhost/echo.pl" >
<!-- Checkbox elements to go here -->
<p>
<input type="submit" value="Submit Form">
</p>
</form>
```

3 Now, in the form element, insert a paragraph containing a checkbox to appear automatically checked
```
<p>Yes, I would like to receive details
<input type="checkbox"
       name="Ask For" value="Details" checked></p>
```

4 Next, in the form element, insert a fieldset containing a legend and five checkboxes to appear unchecked

```
<fieldset>
<legend>Activities of Interest...</legend>
Sailing <input type="checkbox" name="Do" value="Sail">
<br>
Walking <input type="checkbox" name="Do" value="Walk">
<br>
Driving <input type="checkbox" name="Do" value="Drive">
<br>
Ski-ing <input type="checkbox" name="Do" value="Ski">
<br>
Jogging <input type="checkbox" name="Do" value="Jog">
</fieldset>
```

Notice that the **checked** attribute need have no assigned value – its mere presence sets the switch to "on", and its absence leaves the switch in its default "off" state.

5 Save the HTML document, then open the web page in your browser, check some boxes, and submit the form

As the checkboxes for the Walking and Jogging activities are unchecked, their name=value pairs are not sent to the server.

Choosing radio buttons

An HTML5 form can provide visual "radio button" groups, from which the user can select one button to include its associated data for submission to the server. When the button is selected, its switch is set to "on" and its name=value pair will be submitted, otherwise its switch is set to "off" and its name=value pair is not submitted. Unlike checkboxes, radio buttons that share a common name are mutually exclusive, so when one radio button is selected, all others in that group are automatically switched off.

A radio button is created by assigning the value "radio" to the **type** attribute of an **<input>** tag. This tag must also include a **name** attribute and a **value** attribute to specify the name=value pair values. Optionally, this tag may also include a Boolean **checked** attribute to set the initial state of the switch to "on" – so the button will automatically appear selected.

Radio button groups that share a common name can be visually grouped by surrounding their **<input>** elements by **<fieldset> </fieldset>** tags. These may also contain **<legend> </legend>** tags to contain a group name:

radio.html

1 Start a new HTML5 document
```
<!DOCTYPE HTML>
<html lang="en">
<head>
<meta charset="UTF-8">
<title>Radio Button Example</title>
</head>
<body> <!-- Content to go here --> </body>
</html>
```

2 In the body section, insert a form element containing a submit button to send form data by the GET method
```
<form method="GET" action="http://localhost/echo.pl" >
<p>Choose only one answer...</p>
<!-- Fieldset to go here -->
<p> <input type="submit" value="Submit Form"> </p>
</form>
```

3 Next, in the form element, insert a fieldset with a legend
```
<fieldset>
<legend>What kind of language is HTML?</legend>
<!-- Radio button elements to go here -->
</fieldset>
```

4 Now, in the fieldset, insert radio buttons with one selected

Scripting <input type="radio"
  **name="Definition" value="Scripting">
**
Markup <input type="radio"
  **name="Definition" value="Markup">
**
Programming <input type="radio"
name="Definition" value="Programming" checked>

Always include a **checked** attribute to automatically select one button in each radio button group – to provide a default choice.

5 Save the HTML document, then open the web page, select the correct answer, and submit the form

Radio button elements resemble the buttons on old radios where each button selected a particular radio station – but, of course, no two stations could be selected simultaneously.

Selecting options

An HTML5 form can provide a select option list, from which the user can select one option to include its associated data for submission to the server.

A select option list is created using **<select> </select>** tags. The opening **<select>** tag must include a **name** attribute specifying a list name. The **<select>** element encloses **<option> </option>** tags that define each option. Each opening **<option>** tag must include a **value** attribute specifying an option value. When the form is submitted, the list name and the selected option value are sent to the server as a name=value pair.

Optionally, one **<option>** tag may also include a Boolean **selected** attribute to automatically select that option, and the **<option>** elements may be grouped by enclosure in **<optgroup> </optgroup>** tags. The opening **<optgroup>** tag may specify an option group name to a **label** attribute.

A select option list will normally appear as a single-line drop-down list, unless a **size** attribute is included in the **<select>** tag to specify the number of rows to be visible:

select.html

1 Start a new HTML5 document
```
<!DOCTYPE HTML>
<html lang="en">
<head>
<meta charset="UTF-8">
<title>Select Option Example</title>
</head>
<body> <!-- Content to go here --> </body>
</html>
```

2 In the body section, insert a form element containing a submit button to send form data by the GET method
```
<form method="GET" action="http://localhost/echo.pl" >
<!-- Select option lists to go here -->
<p>
<input type="submit" value="Submit Form">
</p>
</form>
```

3 Now, in the form element, insert a fixed height select option list with one option automatically selected

```
<select name="HTML List Type Selector One" size="4">
<optgroup label="List Type 1">
<option value="UL">Unordered List</option>
<option value="OL" selected>Ordered List</option>
<option value="DL">Definition List</option>
</optgroup>
</select>
```

4 Next, in the form element, insert a drop-down select option list with one option automatically selected

```
<select name="HTML List Type Selector Two">
<optgroup label="List Type 2">
<option value="UL">Unordered List</option>
<option value="OL">Ordered List</option>
<option value="DL" selected>Definition List</option>
</optgroup>
</select>
```

Always include a **selected** attribute to automatically select one option in each option list – to provide a default choice.

5 Save the HTML document, then open the web page in your browser, open the drop-down list and submit the form to see the default option values get submitted

Utilizing hidden data

An HTML5 form can provide hidden elements, which create no visible controls but allow additional data to be submitted to the server. Hidden form data is created by assigning the value "hidden" to the **type** attribute of an **<input>** tag. This tag must also include a **name** attribute, and may include a **value** attribute to specify static data that will be submitted as a name=value pair. Optionally, the **<input>** tag may include an **id** attribute and omit the **value** attribute so its value can be specified by script.

Hidden form data can also be used to perform a calculation and dynamically display the result in an **<output> </output>** element. The **<output>** tag must include an **id** attribute and a **for** attribute for reference in script. The **for** attribute can specify multiple element identities as a space separated list. These can be used in an assignment to the **<form>** tag's **oninput** attribute, to perform a calculation whose result will appear in the **<output> </output>** element – but will not be submitted to the server:

hidden.html

Hot tip

Hidden data elements can be useful to maintain user data across a website – a user name entered on the first page can be recalled on any other page.

1 Start a new HTML5 document that incorporates a script

```
<!DOCTYPE HTML>
<html lang="en">
<head>
<meta charset="UTF-8">
<title>Hidden Data Example</title>
<script src="hidden.js"> </script>
</head>
<body> <!-- Content to go here --> </body>
</html>
```

2 In the body section, insert an image with sale price details

```
<img src="sale.png" width="200" height="120" alt="Sale">
```

3 Next, insert a form element to send form data by the GET method

```
<form method="GET" action="http://localhost/echo.pl" >
<!-- Hidden data, input, and output to go here -->
<input type="submit" name="Offer"
        value="Buy Teddy Bears">
</form>
```

4 Within the form element, insert a visible input element for user-entered data

```
Qty (60 Available) <input type="number" id="qty"
name="Quantity" size="2" min="1" max="60">
```

...cont'd

5 Next, in the form element, insert an invisible element for hidden data and an element to display a calculated result
```
<input type="hidden" id="price"
        name="Unit Price" value="24.99">
<output name="sum" for="qty price"></output> <br>
```

Beware

JavaScript is case-sensitive, so you must use the correct case when copying script examples.

6 Now, insert another attribute in the **<form>** tag
```
oninput="sum.value=multiply( qty, price )"
```

7 Create a script to perform the calculation
```
function multiply( q, p )
{
  var result=parseFloat( q.value ) * parseFloat( p.value ) :
  if ( isNaN( result ) || result < 1 ) return "" ;
else return "Total: $" + result.toFixed( 2 ) ;
  }
```

hidden.js

8 Save the HTML document and script, then open the web page in your browser, enter data, and submit the form

159

Don't forget

The hidden form **<input>** data gets submitted to the server but the **<output>** element merely displays the result of the calculation.

Pushing buttons

An HTML5 form can provide push buttons for scripting purposes. When the user pushes a button, a "click event" occurs to which a script function can respond. This allows the user to dynamically interact with the form and can be used to set attribute values. When a script designates a function to be called, whenever a button gets pushed it is said to attach a "behavior" to that button. A push button is created by specifying a "button" value to the **type** attribute of an **<input>** tag, and should also include an **id** attribute so the script can easily identify that element.

Additionally, any HTML5 form can be returned to its original state by pushing a reset button that is created by specifying a "reset" value to the **type** attribute of an **<input>** tag:

button.html

1 Start a new HTML5 document that incorporates a script
```
<!DOCTYPE HTML>
<html lang="en">
<head>
<meta charset="UTF-8">
<title>Button Example</title>
<script src="button.js"> </script>
</head>
<body> <!-- Content to go here --> </body>
</html>
```

2 In the body section, insert a form element containing a reset button, a push button, and a submit button to send form data by the GET method
```
<form method="GET" action="http://localhost/echo.pl" >
<!-- Fieldset to go here -->
<input type="reset" value="Reset Form">
<input type="button" value="Choose For Me" id="btn">
<input type="submit" value="Submit Form">
</form>
```

3 Within the form element, insert a fieldset containing a legend and a checkbox group
```
<fieldset>
<legend>Pizza Toppings</legend>
<input id="pepperoni" type="checkbox"
  name="Toppings" value="Pepperoni"> Pepperoni |
<input id="mushroom" type="checkbox"
  name="Toppings" value="Mushroom"> Mushroom |
<input id="bbqsauce" type="checkbox"
  name="Toppings" value="BBQ Sauce"> BBQ Sauce
</fieldset>
```

4 Create a script that designates a function when the page gets loaded to attach a behavior to the form's push button

function choose()
{ document.getElementById("pepperoni").checked=true ; }

function init()
{ document.getElementById("btn").onclick=choose ; }

onload=init;

button.js

5 Save the HTML document and script, then open the web page in your browser, and push the button to check a box

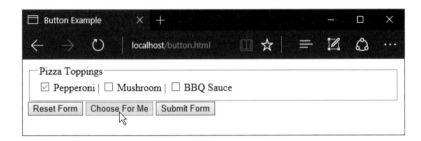

6 Now, push the reset button to clear the form, then check the other two boxes and submit the form

The mere presence of a Boolean **checked** attribute in an HTML element checks the box, but in script, the box's **checked** property needs to be assigned a **true** value to check the box.

Using images for submission

An HTML5 form can use an image button to submit the form, in place of a regular submit button. An image button is created by specifying an "image" value to the **type** attribute of an **<input>** tag and including an **alt** attribute. When a form is submitted by an image button, the XY coordinates of the point at which the click occurred are automatically submitted as name=value pairs along with the rest of the form data.

Additionally, a regular **<img>** tag can be used as an image button by attaching a behavior with script. Where the behavior is to submit a form, the script function can usefully incorporate validation. For example, to ensure a user-entered email address is in the expected format:

ibutton.html

Note that the image button that will perform validation is given an identity so script can attach a behavior to it.

1 Start a new HTML5 document that incorporates a script
```
<!DOCTYPE HTML>
<html lang="en">
<head>
<meta charset="UTF-8">
<title>Image Button Example</title>
<script src="ibutton.js"> </script>
</head>
<body> <!-- Content to go here --> </body>
</html>
```

2 In the body section, insert a form element containing a text input field, which both have an identity for scripting
```
<form id="form-1"
        method="GET" action="http://localhost/echo.pl" >
Please Supply Your Email Address:
<input id="adr"
        name="Address" type="text" size="45"> <br>
<!-- Image Buttons to go here -->
</form>
```

3 Next, in the form element, insert an image button that will simply submit the form
```
<input type="image" src="ibutton.png"
  alt="Submit Button" title="Click to submit form">
```

4 Now, in the form element, insert an image button that will perform validation then submit the form
```
<img id="btn" src="ibutton.png" alt="Submit Button"
  title="Click to submit with JavaScript validation">
```

5 Create a script that designates a function when the page gets loaded – to attach a behavior to an image button

```
function send()
{
  var address = document.getElementById("adr").value ;
  var pattern=
  /^([a-zA-Z0-9_.-])+@([a-zA-Z0-9_.-])+\.([a-zA-Z])+([a-zA-Z])+/ ;
  if( ! pattern.test(address) ) alert("Invalid Email Address") ;
  else document.getElementById("form-1").submit() ;
}

function init()
{ document.getElementById("btn").onclick=send ; }

onload=init;
```

ibutton.js

6 Save the HTML document and script, then open the web page in your browser, enter an incomplete email address and submit the form using each button

7 When validation fails using the button with scripted behavior, complete the email address correctly then use the validating button again to submit the form successfully

The script in this example checks the input text against a regular expression pattern that describes the format of any valid email address. The pattern must appear on a single line – exactly as it is listed here.

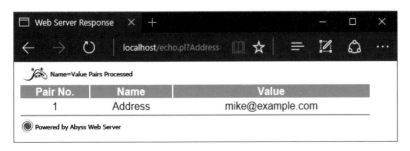

Adding logos to buttons

HTML5 can create push buttons that display small "logo" images using **<button>** **</button>** tags. These tags can then enclose an **<img>** element specifying the URL of the logo image, and text that will appear on the face of the button. Each **<button>** tag should include a **type** attribute to specify whether the button is simply a scripting "button" type, a "submit" form type, or a "reset" form type. Scripting buttons can include an **onclick** attribute in the **<button>** tag to specify the function to be called when the button gets clicked, or directly specify a snippet of script to execute:

logo.html

1 Start a new HTML5 document
```
<!DOCTYPE HTML>
<html lang="en">
<head>
<meta charset="UTF-8">
<title>Logo Button Example</title>
</head>
<body> <!-- Content to go here --> </body>
</html>
```

2 In the body section, insert a form element containing a fieldset with a legend and a text input field
```
<form method="GET" action="http://localhost/echo.pl">
<fieldset>
<legend>Favorite Color</legend>
<input type="text" name="Color">
<!-- Logo Buttons to go here -->
</fieldset>
</form>
```

3 In the fieldset, insert a scripting logo button specifying a snippet of script to execute when that button gets clicked
```
<button type="button"
onclick="alert('Enter your favorite color in the text box')">
<!-- Logo Image and Face Text to go here --> </button>
```

4 Now, within the button element, insert an image element and text that will appear on the face of the button
```
<img src="logo-help.png" alt="Help">Help
```

5 Next, add a button element to submit the form
```
<button type="submit">
<img src="logo-submit.png" alt="Submit">
Submit</button>
```

...cont'd

6 Finally, add a button element to reset the form
```
<button type="reset">
<img src="logo-reset.png" alt="Reset">Reset</button>
```

7 Save the HTML document, then open the web page in your browser and click the "Help" button

You can specify a default value for a text input to the **value** attribute of its **<input>** tag.

8 Enter a color in the text box, then click the reset logo button to clear the text box

9 Enter a color in the text box again then submit the form

Pair No.	Name	Value
1	Color	Aquamarine

Powered by Abyss Web Server

Labeling form controls

Text that is to be associated with an HTML5 form control can be enclosed between **<label>** **</label>** tags. The opening **<label>** tag can include a **for** attribute to specify the value assigned to the control's **id** attribute to make the association. Alternatively, the **<label>** element can simply enclose both the text and the control element to make the association. This allows styling to be applied to the entire label – including the text and control. Often this is useful to distinguish the control associated with particular text.

Additionally, each form control element may include a **tabindex** attribute to specify its tabbing order within the document as a unique value between 0 and 32,767. Using the tab key, the user can then navigate through the document starting at the lowest **tabindex** value and proceeding through successively higher values:

label.html

A form "control" is any **<input>**, **<button>** or **<textarea>** element. A **tabindex** attribute can be included in these tags and also in any **<a>**, **<area>**, **<object>** or **<select>** tag.

1 Start a new HTML5 document with a link element pointing to a style sheet

```
<!DOCTYPE HTML>
<html lang="en">
<head>
<meta charset="UTF-8"> <title>Label Example</title>
<link rel="stylesheet" href="label.css">
</head>
<body> <!-- Content to go here --> </body>
</html>
```

2 In the body section, insert a form element containing a fieldset with a legend

```
<form method="GET" action="http://localhost/echo.pl">
<fieldset>
<legend>Toolbox</legend>
<!-- Form Controls to go here -->
</fieldset>
</form>
```

3 Now, in the fieldset, insert labels that each contain text and a checkbox with a specified tab order

```
<label>Hammer
<input type="checkbox" name="Toolbox"
        value="Hammer" tabindex="2" checked></label>
<label>Wrench
<input type="checkbox" name="Toolbox"
        value="Wrench" tabindex="3"></label>

<!-- Three similar for tabindex 4,5,6 go here -->
```

4 Next, in the fieldset, insert a logo submit button – to be first in the tab order
```
<button type="submit" tabindex="1">
<img src="toolbox.png">Submit</button>
```

5 Save the HTML document then open the web page in your browser to see the text-control association is unclear

6 Edit the HTML document to add a class attribute to each alternate label tag for styling purposes
```
<label class="hilite">
```

7 Create a style sheet with a rule to distinguish the labels
```
label.hilite { background : red ; color : white ; }
```

label.css

8 Save the HTML document and style sheet, then open the web page to see that the text-control association is now clear. Use the tab key to move between controls, and the space bar to select checkboxes, then submit the form

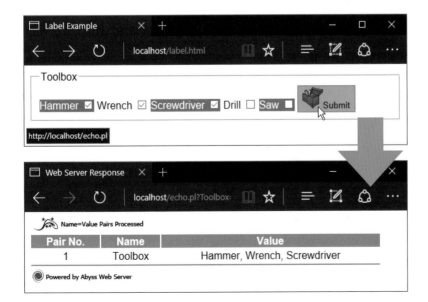

Listing data options

A simple "autocomplete" feature can be provided for a text **<input>** using a **<datalist> </datalist>** element to enclose a number of pre-defined **<option>** values. The user may choose any one of the options, or enter text directly into the input field. In order to associate the **<input>** field with the list, the **<datalist>** tag must include an **id** attribute to specify a list name. The same name must then be specified to a **list** attribute within the **<input>** tag to create the association. The **<input>** tag must also include a name attribute to send to the server as usual.

datalist.html

Don't forget

The name=value pair submitted to the server is the specified list name and the input value selected from the options or entered directly by the user.

1 Start a new HTML5 document with a link element pointing to a style sheet
```
<!DOCTYPE HTML>
<html lang="en">
<head>
<meta charset="UTF-8"> <title>Data List Example</title>
</head>
<body> <!-- Content to go here --> </body>
</html>
```

2 In the body section, insert a form element containing a submit button to send form data by the GET method
```
<form method="GET" action="http://localhost/echo.pl">
<!-- Form data list and input field to go here -->
<p><input type="submit" value="Submit Form"></p>
</form>
```

3 Next, insert a data list of pre-defined options with a specified **id** name
```
<datalist id="browsers"
<option value="Chrome">
<option value="Firefox">
<option value="Internet Explorer">
<option value="Opera">
<option value="Safari">
<option value="Microsoft Edge">
</datalist>
```

4 Now, insert a label that contains text and an input field that is associated with the data list above
```
<label>Choose your browser from this list:
<input list="browsers" name="myBrowser">
</label>
```

5 Save the HTML document, then open the web page in your browser and select the input field to see the pre-defined options appear in a drop-down list

You may need to double-click the input field to override your browsers' own autocomplete suggestions.

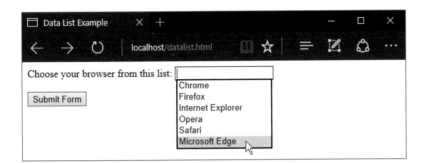

6 Select any option from the drop-down list, or type your own text into the input field to create a value

7 Submit the form to send the input field name and your chosen value to the server

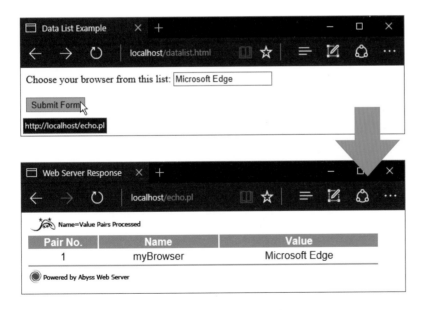

Uploading files

An HTML5 form can provide a file selection facility, which calls upon the operating system's "Choose File" dialog, to allow the user to browse their local file system and select a file.

A file selection facility is created by assigning the value "file" to the **type** attribute of an **<input>** tag, and a name to its **name** attribute. This element produces a text field and a "Browse" button to launch the Choose File dialog. After a file has been selected, its full path appears in the text field. When the form is submitted, the element name and the selected file's name are sent to the web server as a name=value pair.

Where a selected file is to be uploaded to the web server, the **<form>** tag must include an **enctype** attribute specifying the encoding type as "multipart/form-data". Also, its **method** attribute must specify the POST method – because Form Data cannot be appended to a URL using the GET method:

upload.html

1 Start a new HTML5 document
```
<!DOCTYPE HTML>
<html lang="en">
<head>
<meta charset="UTF-8">
<title>File Upload Example</title>
</head>
<body> <!-- Content to go here --> </body>
</html>
```

2 In the body section, insert a form element containing a submit button to send form data by the POST method and specify the encoding type for Form Data
```
<form method="POST" action="http://localhost/upload.pl"
        enctype="multipart/form-data">
<!-- File input element to go here -->
<input type="submit" value="Submit Form">
</form>
```

3 In the form element, insert a file element and a line break
```
<input type="file" name="Upload"> <br>
```

4 Save the HTML document, then open the web page in your browser, select a file and submit the form

To process this example, the files **upload.pl** and **upload.css** need to be added to the "htdocs" directory of a local running web server – these are located in the download archive for this book available from www.ineasysteps. com/resource-centre/ downloads/

5 Examine the headers to see the file details as Form Data

Summary

- HTML5 forms submit data to the web server as name=value pairs for processing by a specified server-side script.

- All form component elements are enclosed between **<form>** **</form>** tags, which must include an **action** attribute, to specify the URL of the processing script, and a **method** attribute to specify the submission method as "GET" or "POST".

- Each **<input>** tag's **type** attribute specifies its component type, such as "text", "password", "checkbox", "radio", etc.

- An **<input>** tag can include **name** and **value** attributes to specify data for submission as a name=value pair.

- An **<input>** tag can enforce its completion by including the **required** keyword, but many automatically prohibit submission if the user enters a value that is not permitted.

- A multi-line text field is created by **<textarea>** **</textarea>** tags that require **rows** and **cols** attributes to specify its size.

- Radio button and checkbox inputs only submit their **name** and **value** attribute data if they are checked.

- An option list is created by enclosing a number of **<option>** elements between **<select>** **</select>** tags.

- Option lists can be enclosed between **<optgroup>** **</optgroup>** tags that can specify an option group name to a **label** attribute.

- Forms can contain "hidden" elements that allow static or script-generated data to be submitted to the server for processing.

- A form may be submitted by a regular submit **<input>** element, by an image **<input>** element, or by a **<button>** element.

- Logo images can be added to the button face by enclosing an **<img>** element between **<button>** **</button>** tags.

- Each form control can be enclosed between **<label>** **</label>** tags to visually group them with text for styling purposes.

- An **<input>** tag can include a **list** attribute to associate it with the **id** of a **<datalist>** element to provide pre-defined options.

- When a form is to upload files, the **<form>** tag must include an **enctype** attribute specifying encoding as "multipart/form-data".

9 Painting on canvas

This chapter demonstrates how to dynamically paint images within an HTML5 document using JavaScript.

174   **Generating a canvas**

176   **Painting shapes**

178   **Stroking borders**

180   **Filling options**

182   **Writing text**

184   **Drawing lines**

186   **Swerving curves**

188   **Translating coordinates**

190   **Transforming shapes**

192   **Animating the canvas**

194   **Summary**

Generating a canvas

In HTML5, the **<canvas> </canvas>** tags create a bitmap canvas area on the page in which script can paint shapes and text. This can be used to dynamically generate graphs, game graphics and visual images.

Initially, the canvas area is invisible and will, by default, be 300 pixels wide and 150 pixels high. Alternative dimensions can be specified to the **<canvas>** element's **width** and **height** attributes.

Optionally, fallback text can be included between the **<canvas> </canvas>** tags that will only be displayed by the browser in the event that the canvas area cannot be created.

In order to use the canvas, a script must first create a "CanvasRenderingContext2D" object. This snappily-named context object provides all the methods and properties needed to paint shapes and text in the canvas area. The context object is created using a **getContext()** method of the canvas itself. For example, for a **<canvas>** element with an **id** of "canvas", like this:

```
var canvas = document.getElementById( "canvas" ) ;
var context = canvas.getContext( "2d" ) ;
```

It is, however, good practice to first test for the existence of the canvas's **getContext()** method before creating the context object:

```
var canvas = document.getElementById( "canvas" ) ;
if ( canvas.getContext ) {  var context = canvas.getContext( "2d" ) ; }
```

Calls to the context object's methods, and assignments to its properties, can subsequently be added inside the **{ }** braces – to be implemented when the test succeeds.

A context object's **fillStyle** property can be assigned a color with which to paint a shape. For example, the context object's **fillRect()** method can be called to paint a rectangle with the assigned color. This method requires four comma-separated "arguments" within its **( )** parentheses – to specify the XY coordinate position on the canvas of the top left corner of the rectangle, its width, and its height:

context.fillRect (*x* , *y*, *width* , *height*) ;

Similarly, the context object's **clearRect()** method can be called to remove paint in a rectangle specified by the same four arguments:

context.clearRect (*x* , *y*, *width* , *height*) ;

Beware

JavaScript is case-sensitive, so be sure to capitalize the **fillRect** and **clearRect** method names correctly – capital "R".

Don't forget

Canvas coordinates have their XY origin at their top left corner – so **fillRect(100,10, 50,50)** would paint a 50 pixel square 100 pixels from the left edge of the canvas and 10 pixels down from its top edge.

1 Start a new HTML5 document that incorporates a script and creates a canvas area of a specified size

```
<!DOCTYPE HTML>
<html lang="en">
<head>
<meta charset="UTF-8">
<title>Canvas Example</title>
<script src="canvas.js"></script>
</head>
<body>
<canvas id="canvas" width="550" height="150">
[Fallback Message]
</canvas>
</body>
</html>
```

canvas.html

2 Create a script with a function to paint the entire canvas area a specified color, then remove a 100-pixel square at specified coordinates, as soon as the document has loaded

```
function init()
{
  var canvas = document.getElementById( "canvas" ) ;
  if ( canvas.getContext )
  {
    var ctx = canvas.getContext( "2d" ) ;
    ctx.fillStyle = "#F30" ;
    ctx.fillRect ( 0, 0, canvas.width , canvas.height ) ;
    ctx.clearRect( 225, 25, 100,100 ) ;
  }
}
onload = init ;
```

canvas.js

Name the context object variable "ctx" for brevity, as it will be typed often.

3 Save the HTML document and script, then open the web page in your browser to see the painted canvas area

175

Painting shapes

The three basic shapes that can be painted on an HTML5 canvas are rectangle, circle and polygon. A rectangle is the simplest shape to create using the context object's **fillRect()** method, introduced in the previous example on pages 174-175, that has this syntax:

ctx.fillRect (*x, y, width, height*) ;

Creating circles and polygons requires a little more effort, as they must both be initially created as a "path" describing the shape. The path of a circle describes the coordinates of its center point and its radius, and the path of a triangle describes the coordinates of each of its corners. A path always begins with a call to the context object's **beginPath()** method – announcing the creation of a path.

A circular path is created with the context object's **arc()** method whose arguments first describe the coordinates of its center point and its radius. Additionally, because this method can also be used to create a partial circle, further arguments describe the start angle, end angle, and the direction in which to paint:

ctx.arc (*x, y, radius, startAngle, endAngle, direction*) ;

Sadly, the start and end angles must be specified in "radians", rather than degrees, but degrees can easily be converted to radians using the expression *degrees****Math.PI/180**. A complete circle of 360 degrees can, therefore, start at zero and end at **360*Math.PI/180**, more simply expressed as just **Math.PI*2**. The final argument to the context object's **arc()** method, describing the direction in which to paint, is a Boolean value of either **true** or **false** – where **false** is clockwise and **true** is counterclockwise.

A polygonal path is created with the context object's **moveTo()** and **lineTo()** methods that both require two XY coordinate arguments. Initially, the **moveTo()** method describes the point at which to begin the path, like lifting a pen off paper and moving to a new point at which to begin drawing. Successive calls to the **lineTo()** method then describe each corner point along the edge of the shape. Finally, a call to the context object's **closePath()** method completes the path shape by returning to its starting point.

After creating a circular or polygonal path, a simple call to the context object's **fill()** method will paint the shape with the color specified to the context object's current **fillStyle** property.

The context object's **closePath()** and **fill()** methods both require no arguments.

The expression **Math.PI** can be used for a radians value equivalent to 180 degrees – a half circle.

1 Create a script with a function to paint a 100-pixel square as soon as the document has loaded

```
function init()
{
  var canvas = document.getElementById( "canvas" ) ;
  if ( canvas.getContext )
  {
    var ctx = canvas.getContext( "2d" ) ;
    ctx.fillStyle = "#F30" ;
    ctx.fillRect ( 75, 10, 100 , 100 ) ;
    /* More instructions go here */
  }
}
onload = init ;
```

shapes.js

2 Next, insert instructions to paint a 50-pixel radius circle

```
ctx.fillStyle = "#3C0" ;
ctx.beginPath() ;
ctx.arc( 275, 60, 50, 0, Math.PI*2, true ) ;
ctx.fill() ;
```

3 Now, insert instructions to paint a 100-pixel tall triangle

```
ctx.fillStyle = "#09F" ;
ctx.beginPath() ;
ctx.moveTo( 375, 110 ) ;
ctx.lineTo( 425,10 ) ; ctx.lineTo( 475,110 ) ;
ctx.closePath() ;
ctx.fill() ;
```

4 Save the script alongside an HTML document that incorporates this script and creates a canvas with the **id** value of "canvas" (just like the one listed on page 175)

shapes.html

5 Open the web page in your browser to see the shapes get painted on the canvas

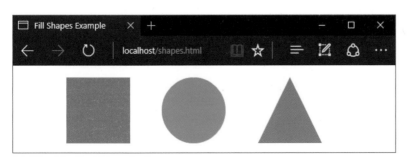

Stroking borders

Just as a context object provides a **fillStyle** property, **fillRect()** and **fill()** methods, which can be used to paint a shape, it also provides a **strokeStyle** property, **strokeRect()** and **stroke()** methods that can be used to paint borders.

The blue border shown here has 50% fill transparency to illustrate the overlap – setting fill transparency is described in the next example on pages 180-181.

A context object's **strokeStyle** property can be assigned a color with which to paint the borders. The context object's **strokeRect()** method requires four comma-separated arguments within its ( ) parentheses – to specify the XY coordinate position on the canvas of the top left corner of a rectangle, its width and its height:

ctx.strokeRect (x, y, width, height) ;

Circular and polygonal borders are painted by first creating a path, as described in the previous example on pages 176-177, then calling the context object's **stroke()** method.

Before painting a border, however, it is necessary to first specify a numeric pixel value to the context object's **lineWidth** property – to determine what brush width to use.

It should be noted that the border is painted in the specified **lineWidth** <u>centered</u> on the path – half outside and half inside. For example, with a **lineWidth** value of 20 pixels, the border gets painted with 10 pixels on each side of the path:

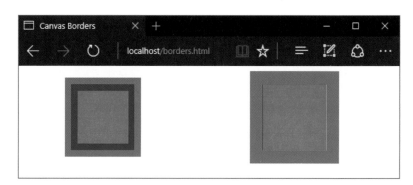

In order to paint a border entirely outside an existing fill path, the stroke path width and height needs to be increased by the **lineWidth** value, and the XY coordinates need to be reduced by half the **lineWidth** value. For example, where the **lineWidth** value is 20 and the fill is created by **ctx.fillRect(20, 20, 100, 100)**, an external border is created by **ctx.strokeRect(10, 10, 120, 120)**.

1 Create a script with a function to paint a 6-pixel wide border centered on a 100-pixel square path

```
function init()
{
  var canvas = document.getElementById( "canvas" ) ;
  if ( canvas.getContext )
  {
    var ctx = canvas.getContext( "2d" ) ;
    ctx.lineWidth = 6 ; ctx.strokeStyle = "#F30" ;
    ctx.strokeRect ( 75, 10, 100, 100 ) ;
    /* More instructions go here */
  }
}
onload = init ;
```

stroke.js

2 Next, insert instructions to paint a circular border

```
ctx.strokeStyle =" #3C0" ;
ctx.beginPath() ;
ctx.arc( 275, 60, 50, 0, Math.PI*2, true ) ;
ctx.stroke() ;
```

3 Now, insert instructions to paint a triangular border

```
ctx.strokeStyle = "#09F" ;
ctx.beginPath() ;
ctx.moveTo( 375, 110 ) ;
ctx.lineTo( 425, 10 ) ; ctx.lineTo( 475,110 ) ;
ctx.closePath() ;
ctx.stroke() ;
```

4 Save the script alongside an HTML document that incorporates this script and creates a canvas with the **id** value of "canvas" (just like the one listed on page 175)

stroke.html

5 Open the web page in your browser to see the borders get painted on the canvas

179

Hot tip

Should you want to paint a lot of shapes with the same fill transparency, you can specify a value in the range of 0.0-1.0 to the context object's **globalAlpha** property. For example, set a 50% transparency with **ctx.globalAlpha=0.5**.

Don't forget

Do not simply specify the URL of an image as the first argument to the **createPattern()** method.

Filling options

Fill and stroke colors can be specified to a context object's **fillStyle** and **strokeStyle** properties as a recognized color name, such as "red", or as a hexadecimal value, such as "#FF0000" or its shorthand equivalent "#F00". Additionally, colors can be specified by stating their red, green, and blue component values in the range 0-255 with an **rgb()** expression. For example, the color red can be expressed as **rgb(255,0,0)** – having maximum red component value but no green or blue. The fill color's transparency can also be specified in the range 0.0-1.0 as the fourth argument in an **rgba()** expression. For example, the expression **rgba(255,0,0,0.5)** specifies maximum red of 50% transparency.

Alternatively, a context object's **fillStyle** and **strokeStyle** properties can be assigned a "CanvasGradient" object that defines a multi-color gradient fill, in which one color gradually changes to another. To create a CanvasGradient object, the context object provides two methods. The **createLinearGradient()** method requires four arguments to specify two XY coordinates at which to start and end a linear gradient. For example, **createLinearGradient(0,0,100,100)** defines a diagonal gradient from top left to bottom right. The **createRadialGradient()** method requires six arguments to specify two XY coordinates and two radius values at which to start and end a radial gradient. For example, **createRadialGradient(50,50,10,50,50,100)** defines a radial gradient between two circles centered at the same point.

Each CanvasGradient object has an **addColorStop()** method that requires two arguments to specify the position along the gradient in the range 0.0-1.0, and the color to paint at that position. For example, **addColorStop(0,"red")** begins the gradient fill with red, and **addColorStop(1,"blue")** ends the gradient fill with blue.

A context object's **fillStyle** and **strokeStyle** properties can alternatively be assigned a "CanvasPattern" object that defines a pattern image and how it should be repeated. To create a CanvasPattern object, the context object provides a **createPattern()** method. This requires two arguments specifying a loaded Image object and a repetition value of "repeat-x" (horizontal), "repeat-y" (vertical), or "repeat" (both). The Image object is created using the JavaScript **new Image()** constructor and the URL of an image to be used by the pattern assigned to its **src** property. The pattern can then be applied after the image has loaded.

...cont'd

1 Create a script with a function to paint colored rectangles

```
function init()
{
  var canvas = document.getElementById( "canvas" ) ;
  if ( canvas.getContext )
  {
    var ctx = canvas.getContext( "2d" ) ;
    ctx.fillStyle = "rgb( 255, 51, 0 )" ;
    ctx.fillRect ( 50, 10, 80, 80 ) ;
    ctx.fillStyle = "rgba( 0, 153, 255, 0.5 )" ;
    ctx.fillRect( 100, 30, 80, 80 ) ;
    /*  More instructions go here */
  }
} onload = init ;
```

options.js

2 Next, insert instructions to paint gradient-filled rectangles

```
var linear = ctx.createLinearGradient( 0, 10, 0, 110 ) ;
linear.addColorStop( 0 , "yellow" ) ;
linear.addColorStop( 1 , "green" ) ;
ctx.fillStyle = linear ; ctx.fillRect( 200, 10, 100, 100 ) ;
var radial = ctx.createRadialGradient( 370, 60, 0, 370, 60, 70 ) ;
radial.addColorStop( 0 , "yellow" ) ;
radial.addColorStop( 1 , "green" ) ;
ctx.fillStyle = radial ; ctx.fillRect( 320, 10, 100, 100 ) ;
```

3 Now, insert instructions to paint a pattern-filled rectangle

```
var image = new Image() ; image.src = "options.png" ;
image.onload = function( ) {
var pattern = ctx.createPattern( image, "repeat" ) ;
ctx.fillStyle = pattern ; ctx.fillRect( 440, 10, 100, 100 ) ; } ;
```

4 Save the script alongside an HTML document that incorporates this script and creates a canvas with the **id** value of "canvas" (just like the one listed on page 175)

options.html

5 Open the web page in your browser to see the fill options

options.png 32px x 32px

Writing text

Text can be written on an HTML5 canvas using the context object's **fillText()** and/or **strokeText()** methods. These each require three arguments to specify the text to be written, enclosed within quote marks, and the XY coordinates at which to place the bottom left corner of the text on the canvas. The text will appear painted in the canvas object's current **fillStyle** and/or **strokeStyle**.

The font in which to write the text can first be specified to the context object's **font** property. This accepts values in the same serial format as the CSS font shorthand property – to specify the font style, weight, size, and family. For example, the instruction **ctx.font = "italic bold 90px Fantasy"** specifies an italic style, bold weight, 90-pixel size, and the "Fantasy" font family. Optionally, each value may be omitted from the series, so to simply specify an italic font style, the instruction could read **ctx.font="italic"**.

The context object can add shadow effects to any shape it paints, but is particularly useful to add drop-shadow effects to text. Shadow color, offset, and blur are specified by the context object's **shadowColor, shadowOffsetX, shadowOffsetY,** and **shadowBlur** properties. Positive **shadowOffsetX** values position the shadow to the right of the text, and positive **shadowOffsetY** values position the shadow below the text. Negative values may be specified to position the shadow to the left and above the text respectively:

Don't forget

The XY coordinates specified to **fillRect()** position the top left corner of a rectangle – but those specified to **fillText()** position the text's bottom left corner.

write.js

1 Create a script with a function to paint some bold text
```
function init()
{
  var canvas = document.getElementById( "canvas" ) ;
  if ( canvas.getContext )
  {
    var ctx = canvas.getContext( "2d" ) ;
    ctx.font = "bold 70px Arial, sans-serif" ;
    ctx.fillStyle = "#F30" ;
    ctx.fillText( "HTML5", 10, 60 ) ;
    /*  More instructions go here */
  }
}
onload = init ;
```

2 Next, insert instructions to paint some regular text
```
ctx.font = "32px Arial" ;
ctx.fillStyle = "#09F" ;
ctx.fillText( "with Context 2D", 10, 130 ) ;
```

3 Now, insert instructions to paint outlined text
```
ctx.font = "italic bold 60px Fantasy" ;
ctx.strokeStyle = "#3C0" ;
ctx.strokeText( "Canvas Fun", 10, 100 ) ;
```

4 Specify values for each context object shadow property
```
ctx.shadowOffsetX = 2 ;
ctx.shadowOffsetY = 2 ;
ctx.shadowBlur = 3 ;
ctx.shadowColor = "black" ;
```

5 Finally, insert instructions to paint text that will receive a drop-shadow effect
```
ctx.font = "italic bold 90px Fantasy" ;
ctx.fillStyle = "#FF0" ;
ctx.fillText( "Drop", 310, 60 ) ;
ctx.fillText( "Shadow", 310, 130 ) ;
```

6 Save the script alongside an HTML document that incorporates this script and creates a canvas with the **id** value of "canvas" (just like the one listed on page 175)

write.html

7 Open the web page in your browser to see the text written on the canvas and admire the drop-shadow effect

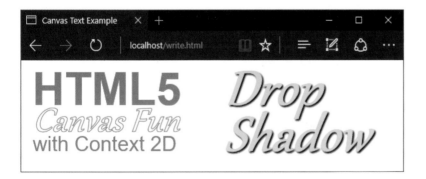

Shadow properties are global, so once values have been specified to them, all further shapes painted onto the canvas will automatically receive a shadow. This can be prevented, however, by assigning a value of "transparent" to the **shadowColor** property.

Drawing lines

Lines are initially created as paths that start with the context object's **beginPath()** method, then use its **moveTo()** and **lineTo()** methods to specify the coordinates on the HTML5 canvas at which to draw the line. A call to the context object's **stroke()** method draws the line using the current **strokeStyle** and **lineWidth**.

By default, the ends of the line are drawn flat, exactly abutting the canvas coordinates, but alternate line endings can be specified to the context object's **lineCap** property. Specifying a "round" value adds a semi-circular cap onto the line endings, and specifying a "square" value adds a rectangular cap. Each cap adds half the line's width. Normal line endings can be resumed by specifying the default "butt" value to the context object's **lineCap** property.

Where two lines join at an angle they will, by default, automatically receive an extension beyond the specified coordinates to create a mitered point. This extends the outer edge of each line until they meet, then fills the triangle formed by the extension. When two lines join at a very acute angle, the extension needed to form the miter triangle can be lengthy, so the context object provides a **miterLimit** property to constrain the extension length. Initially, this property has a value of "10", which is generally desirable, but its value can be changed if necessary.

The extended miter normally created where two lines join can be prevented by specifying a "bevel" value to the context object's **lineJoin** property, or an attractive filled arc can be added to the line ends by specifying a "round" value. Normal line joints can be resumed by specifying the default "miter" value to the context object's **lineJoin** property.

lines.js

1 Create a script with a function to paint a triangle

```
function init()
{
  var canvas = document.getElementById( "canvas" ) ;
  if ( canvas.getContext )
  {
    var ctx = canvas.getContext("2d") ; ctx.lineWidth = 20 ;
    ctx.strokeStyle = "#F30" ; ctx.beginPath() ;
    ctx.moveTo(20,130) ; ctx.lineTo(70,30) ; ctx.lineTo(120,130) ;
    ctx.closePath() ; ctx.stroke() ;
    /*  More instructions go here */
  }
}
onload = init ;
```

2 Next, insert instructions to paint lines with different ends

```
ctx.strokeStyle = "#3C0" ;
ctx.beginPath();
ctx.lineCap = "butt" ;
ctx.moveTo( 160, 30 ) ; ctx.lineTo( 160, 120 ) ; ctx.stroke() ;
ctx.beginPath() ;
ctx.lineCap = "round" ;
ctx.moveTo( 200, 30 ) ; ctx.lineTo( 200, 120 ) ; ctx.stroke() ;
ctx.beginPath() ;
ctx.lineCap = "square" ;
ctx.moveTo( 240, 30 ) ; ctx.lineTo( 240, 120 ) ; ctx.stroke() ;
```

3 Now, insert instructions to paint lines with different joints

```
ctx.strokeStyle = "#09F" ;
ctx.beginPath() ;
ctx.lineJoin = "miter" ;
ctx.moveTo(280,80) ; ctx.lineTo(330,30) ; ctx.lineTo(330,120) ;
ctx.stroke() ;
ctx.beginPath() ;
ctx.lineJoin = "round" ;
ctx.moveTo(370,80) ; ctx.lineTo(420,30) ; ctx.lineTo(420,120) ;
ctx.stroke() ;
ctx.beginPath() ;
ctx.lineJoin = "bevel" ;
ctx.moveTo(460,80) ; ctx.lineTo(510,30) ; ctx.lineTo(510,120) ;
ctx.stroke() ;
```

4 Save the script alongside an HTML document that incorporates this script and creates a canvas with the **id** value of "canvas" (just like the one listed on page 175)

5 Open the web page in your browser to see the lines painted on the canvas and admire their ends and joints

Lines are painted by stroking, but when **closePath()** has been used to create a shape, that shape can be filled.

lines.html

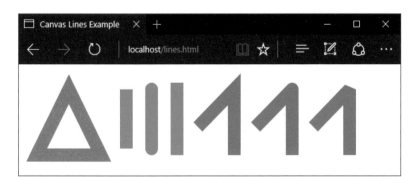

Swerving curves

The context object's **arc()** method, which was used in a previous example on pages 176-177 to paint a complete circle, can be used to paint a curved line on the canvas that is simply part of a circle's circumference. Recall that the **arc()** method requires six arguments to specify the circle's center point, radius, start angle (in radians), end angle (in radians), and the direction in which to paint – with this syntax:

ctx.arc (*x, y, radius, startAngle, endAngle, direction*) ;

When painting a complete circle, the Boolean direction value is irrelevant, but it is important when painting an arc, to determine which part of the circumference is to be painted. For example, when the start angle is at 3 o'clock (zero) and the end angle is at 12 o'clock (**Math.PI/180*270**), painting counterclockwise (**true**) creates an arc that is only one quarter of the circumference, but clockwise (**false**) creates an arc of the other three quarters.

Simple curved lines that are not arcs can be painted on the canvas using the context object's **quadraticCurveTo()** method. This requires four arguments – specifying the XY coordinates of <u>one</u> invisible control point, then the XY coordinates at which the line will end. Similarly, complex curved lines can be painted on the canvas using the context object's **bezierCurveTo()** method. This requires six arguments – specifying the XY coordinates of <u>two</u> invisible control points, then the XY coordinates at which the line will end. In each case, the line gets painted from the current position in the path and swerves towards the control points to create the curve:

The formula to convert degrees to radians is described on page 176.

curves.js

1 Create a script with a function to paint two 100-pixel square rectangles – upon which to paint arcs

```
function init()
{
  var canvas = document.getElementById( "canvas" ) ;
  if ( canvas.getContext )
  {
    var ctx = canvas.getContext( "2d" ) ;
    ctx.lineWidth = 15 ;
    ctx.strokeStyle = "#F30" ;
    ctx.fillStyle = "#FF0" ;
    ctx.fillRect( 70, 20, 100, 100 ) ;
    ctx.fillRect( 200, 20, 100, 100 ) ;
    /*  More instructions go here */
  }
}
onload = init ;
```

2 Next, insert instructions to paint two arcs from the same circumference position, but painted in different directions

```
ctx.beginPath();
ctx.arc( 70, 70, 50, 0, Math.PI/180*90, true ) ;
ctx.stroke() ;
ctx.beginPath() ;
ctx.arc( 120, 70, 50, 0, Math.PI/180*90, false ) ;
ctx.stroke() ;
```

The background rectangles in this example are included to illustrate positioning – paint 1-pixel square rectangles at the control point coordinates (350,100), (550,10), and (450,100) to see how they swerve the curves.

3 Now, insert instructions to paint a filled semi-circle

```
ctx.beginPath() ;
ctx.arc( 250, 70, 50, Math.PI/180*90, Math.PI/180*270, true ) ;
ctx.fillStyle = "#3C0" ; ctx.fill() ;
```

4 Paint a simple curve using one control point

```
ctx.strokeStyle = "#09F" ;
ctx.beginPath() ;
ctx.moveTo( 350, 10 ) ;
ctx.quadraticCurveTo( 350, 100, 440, 100 ) ;
ctx.stroke() ;
```

5 Now, paint a complex curve using two control points

```
ctx.beginPath() ;
ctx.moveTo( 450, 10 ) ;
ctx.bezierCurveTo( 550, 10, 450, 100, 550, 100 ) ;
ctx.stroke() ;
```

187

6 Save the script alongside an HTML document that incorporates this script and creates a canvas with the **id** value of "canvas" (just like the one listed on page 175)

curves.html

7 Open the web page in your browser to see the rectangles, arcs and curves painted on the canvas

The formula to convert degrees to radians is described on page 176.

Translating coordinates

The canvas XY coordinate origin, which by default sets 0,0 at the top left corner of the canvas, can be changed by specifying new XY coordinate origins to the context object's **translate()** method. After painting at the new coordinates, the canvas state can then be saved using the context object's **save()** method, before restoring the initial default origin using the context object's **restore()** method. This technique is especially useful when painting multiple shapes from a script loop to move the canvas on each iteration.

Script loops can also scale shapes on successive iterations, using the context object's **scale()** method. This requires two arguments to specify the "scale factor" in the horizontal and vertical directions. For example, **ctx.scale(0.5, 0.5)** scales down by 50% in each direction, and **ctx.scale(1.5, 1.5)** scales up by 50%.

The context object also provides a **rotate()** method that allows the canvas to be rotated clockwise by the angle (expressed in radians) specified as its single argument. For example, specifying an argument of **Math.Pi*2/36** rotates the canvas 10 degrees (360/36). Script loops can call the context object's **rotate()** method on successive iterations of a loop, to paint shapes in a circular pattern:

translate.js

① Create a script with a function to paint a series of square rectangles – by translating the XY canvas origin on each iteration of a loop

```
function init()
{
  var canvas = document.getElementById( "canvas" ) ;
  if ( canvas.getContext )
  {
    var i, j, ctx = canvas.getContext( "2d" ) ;
    ctx.fillStyle = "#F30" ;
    for( i = 0 ; i < 3 ; i++ )
    {
      for( j = 0 ; j < 3 ; j++ )
      {
          ctx.save() ;
          ctx.translate( 50*j, 50*i ) ;
          ctx.fillRect( 0, 0, 30, 30 ) ;
          ctx.restore() ;
      }
    }
    /*  More instructions go here */
  }
}
onload = init ;
```

...cont'd

2 Next, insert a loop construct to paint a series of rectangles – by translating the XY canvas origin and scaling down on each iteration of the loop

```
ctx.fillStyle = "#3C0" ;
ctx.translate( 150, 0 ) ;
for( i = 0 ; i < 3 ; i++ )
{
  ctx.fillRect( 0, 0, 100, 100 ) ;
  ctx.translate( 110, 0 ) ;
  ctx.scale( 0.75, 0.75 ) ;
}
```

3 Now, insert instructions to paint a series of circles – by rotating the canvas on each iteration of a loop

```
ctx.fillStyle = "#09F" ;
ctx.translate( 180, 120 ) ;
for ( i = 1 ; i < 6 ; i++ )
{
  for ( j = 0 ; j < i*6 ; j++ )
  {
    ctx.rotate( Math.PI*2 / ( i*6 ) ) ;
    ctx.beginPath() ;
    ctx.arc( 0, i*22.5, 8, 0, Math.PI*2, true ) ;
    ctx.fill() ;
  }
}
```

4 Save the script alongside an HTML document that incorporates this script and creates a canvas with the **id** value of "canvas" (just like the one listed on page 175)

5 Open the web page in your browser to see the shapes painted at the various coordinates by the loops

The context accumulates calls to **translate()**, **scale()**, and **rotate()** in a matrix – so after rotating, say, 45 degrees, a subsequent call to **translate()** along the X axis will move diagonally, not horizontally! The next example on pages 190-191, shows how to avoid this by resetting the matrix.

translate.html

transform.js

Transforming shapes

When creating shapes and paths, the context object applies a "transformation matrix" to the canvas coordinates. Initially, this provides an "identity transform" for the context object's methods. For example, it ensures rectangle corner angles are all 90 degrees.

The transformation matrix can be manipulated, however, to allow the context object's methods to behave differently. For example, to create skewed rectangles that do not have 90 degree corners.

Calling a context object's **transform()** method can apply a transformation by multiplying the current matrix values. For example, the call **ctx.transform(1, -0.3, 0, 1, 0, 0)** will skew rectangles when painting. The current matrix retains previous transformations, but usefully can be reset to the default identity matrix with the call **ctx.setTransform(1, 0, 0, 1, 0, 0)** – so previous calls to **rotate()**, **scale()**, **translate()**, and **transform()** are forgotten.

The appearance of shapes can be also be modified by first defining a clipping path to act as a mask. Subsequently, only shapes, or parts of shapes, that are inside the clipping path will be painted.

A clipping path is simply a specified path, created like any other path, that ends with a call to the context object's **clip()** method:

1 Create a script with a function to paint a 100-pixel square rectangle – using the identity transformation matrix

```
function init()
{
  var canvas = document.getElementById( "canvas" ) ;
  if ( canvas.getContext )
  {
    var ctx = canvas.getContext( "2d" ) ;
    ctx.fillStyle = "#F30" ;
    ctx.fillRect( 20, 40, 100, 100 ) ;
    /*  More instructions go here */
  }
}
onload = init ;
```

2 Next, insert instructions to paint a 100-pixel square rectangle – by multiplying the current matrix values

```
ctx.fillStyle = "#3C0" ;
ctx.transform( 1, -0.3, 0, 1, 0, 0 ) ;
ctx.fillRect( 160, 90, 100, 100 ) ;
```

3 Now, insert an instruction to reset to the default identity transformation matrix – forgetting the last transformation
```
ctx.setTransform( 1, 0, 0, 1, 0, 0 ) ;
```

4 Paint another rectangle – once more using the identity transformation matrix
```
ctx.fillStyle = "#09F" ;
ctx.fillRect( 350, 10, 130, 130 ) ;
```

5 Next, create a circular clipping path, centered in the rectangle just painted
```
ctx.beginPath() ;
ctx.arc( 415, 75, 50, 0, Math.PI*2, true ) ;
ctx.clip() ;
```

6 Now, paint two more rectangles over the clipping path
```
ctx.fillStyle = "#FF0" ;
ctx.fillRect( 350, 10, 130, 130 ) ;
ctx.fillStyle = "#F0F" ;
ctx.fillRect( 350, 10, 65, 65 ) ;
```

7 Save the script alongside an HTML document that incorporates this script and creates a canvas with the **id** value of "canvas" (just like the one listed on page 175)

8 Open the web page in your browser to see the skewed rectangle, painted using the modified transformation matrix, and the rectangles clipped by the mask

Consider each canvas element to have, by default, a clipping path that is the same size as the entire canvas – so no clipping occurs.

transform.html

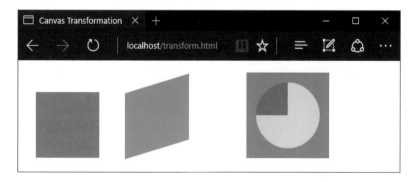

Animating the canvas

Animations can easily be created on a canvas, simply by repeatedly clearing the current canvas then repainting it with shapes at a modified position. A canvas can be repainted faster than the human eye can detect, so animations appear to be very smooth. The fundamental components of a canvas animation script are:

- Initialize a context object and shape starting positions.

- Clear the canvas, then paint shapes onto the canvas.

- Calculate new shape positions for the next repaint.

Where the canvas animation has a static background and border, these can be created as styles so they need not be repeatedly painted onto the canvas:

animate.js

1 Create a script that begins by declaring global variables for the context object, canvas size, XY coordinates, and direction step size
var ctx, w, h, x, y, dx, dy ;

2 Add a function that initializes a context object property and applies styles as soon as the HTML document loads
```
function init()
{
  var canvas = document.getElementById( "canvas" ) ;
  if ( canvas.getContext )
  {
    ctx = canvas.getContext( "2d" ) ;
    ctx.fillStyle = "#F30" ;
    canvas.style.background = "#FF0" ;
    canvas.style.border = "6px solid #09F" ;
    /* More instructions go here */
  }
}
onload = init ;
```

3 Now, insert instructions to initialize the global variables with XY coordinates for the starting position of a "ball", its direction step size, and canvas size
```
x = 5 ; y = 44 ;
dx = 5 ; dy = 5 ;
w = canvas.width ;
h = canvas.height ;
```

4 Insert an instruction to call a function that will calculate new XY coordinates every 25 milliseconds
setInterval(position, 25) ;

5 Next, add the function that calculates new XY coordinates and stores them in global variables – after it first calls a function to actually paint the ball onto the canvas

```
function position()
{
  paint() ;
  if ( ( x+dx > w ) || ( x+dx < 0 ) ) dx = -dx ;
  if ( ( y+dy > h ) || ( y+dy < 0 ) ) dy = -dy ;
  x += dx ;
  y += dy ;
}
```

Hot tip

Notice how the polarity of the direction step gets reversed when the ball collides with a perimeter – so it doesn't bounce right off the canvas.

6 Now, add the function that clears the canvas and actually paints the ball at the current stored XY coordinates

```
function paint( )
{
  ctx.clearRect( 0, 0, w, h ) ;
  ctx.beginPath() ;
  ctx.arc( x, y, 30, 0, Math.PI * 2, true ) ;
  ctx.fill() ;
}
```

7 Save the script alongside an HTML document that incorporates this script and creates a canvas with the **id** value of "canvas" (just like the one listed on page 175)

animate.html

8 Open the web page in your browser to see the animated ball bouncing around the canvas

Summary

- The HTML5 **<canvas>** element creates a bitmap canvas area on a page in which script can paint shapes and text – using the canvas context object's methods and properties.

- A context object's **fillStyle, strokeStyle,** and **lineWidth** properties specify the current fill color, stroke color, and line width.

- A rectangle can be simply painted using the context object's **fillRect()** or **strokeRect()** methods to specify position and size.

- Creating a path always begins by calling the context object's **beginPath()** method, and may be closed with **closePath()**.

- A path may use the context object's **moveTo(), lineTo(),** and **arc()** methods to describe path coordinates, then paint the path on the canvas by calling its **fill()** or **stroke()** methods.

- Fills may also be semi-transparent colors, gradients, or patterns.

- Text painted onto a canvas by the context object's **fillText()** and **strokeText()** methods can be enhanced by a shadow effect.

- A path can specify the appearance of line endings and line joints to the context object's **lineCap** and **lineJoin** properties.

- A context object's **quadraticCurveTo()** and **bezierCurveTo()** methods both specify end point XY coordinates and control point XY coordinates to define curves.

- The context object's **translate()** method changes the canvas XY origin, its **rotate()** method rotates the canvas, and its **scale()** method modifies a shape by a specified scale factor.

- Canvas state can be saved by the context object's **save()** method and the default XY origin restored by its **restore()** method.

- The context object's **transform(), setTransform(),** and **clip()** methods can be used to modify its painting behavior.

- Canvas animation is achieved by repeatedly clearing the canvas and repainting it faster than the human eye can detect.

10 Employing APIs

This chapter demonstrates **196** Measuring fractions

how a document can **198** Dragging and dropping objects

incorporate powerful **200** Manipulating pixels

HTML5 features through **202** Storing user data

Application Programming **204** Editing live content

Interfaces (APIs). **206** Cross-document messaging

208 Pinpointing the user

210 Summary

The **<details>**, **<summary>**, **<menu>** and **<menuitem>** elements are new tags introduced in HTML 5.1.

meter.html

The **<meter>** element should only be used to indicate a fractional measurement within a specified range, not to indicate progress – use the **<progress>** element for that (see page 140).

Measuring fractions

The fundamental Application Programming Interface (API) available in any HTML document is provided by the Document Object Model (DOM). The DOM is a hierarchical object tree, representing all elements and attributes within that document, that can be manipulated by scripting. For example, the **value** attribute in a **<meter>** tag, which defines a fractional measurement in a range specified to its **min** and **max** attributes, can be manipulated by script as the measurement changes.

Interactive **<details>** and **<summary>** elements can respond to user actions without scripting to disclose additional information.

Interactive **<menu>** and **<menuitem>** elements can provide context menu commands to call upon script functions:

1 Create an HTML5 document that incorporates a script, then in the body section insert a fieldset with an associated context menu and containing three checkboxes

```
<script src = "meter.js" > </script>

<fieldset contextmenu="commands">
<input type="checkbox" class="box" onclick="sum()">1
<input type="checkbox" class="box" onclick="sum()">2
<input type="checkbox" class="box" onclick="sum()">3
</fieldset>
```

2 Next, insert the context menu with one command item

```
<menu type="context" id="command">
<menuitem label="Uncheck All" onclick="zero()">
</menu>
```

3 Now, insert a measure of the number of checked boxes within the fieldset

```
<meter id="mtr" value="0" min="0" max="3"></meter>
```

4 Then, add elements to disclose the numeric total of checked boxes within the fieldset

```
<details>
<summary>Number of items Checked</summary>
<span id="num">0</span>
</details>
```

5 Begin a script with a statement to initialize a variable array that references each checkbox
```
var boxes = document.getElementsByClassName( "box" ) ;
```

meter.js

6 Next, add a function to count the number of checked boxes, then display the measure and numeric total
```
function sum() {
var i , num = 0 ;
  for ( i = 0 ; i < boxes.length ; i++ )
  { if ( boxes[ i ].checked ) num++ ; }
  document.getElementById( "mtr" ).value = num ;
  document.getElementById( "num" ).innerHTML = num ;
}
```

7 Finally, add a function to uncheck all checkboxes then display the zeroed measure and numeric total
```
function zero() {
  var i = 0 ;
  while ( i < boxes.length )
  { boxes[ i ].checked = false ; i++ ; }
  sum() ;
}
```

The **<details>** element is somewhat experimental and may disclose details in a drop-down box that appears when you click an arrow button.

8 Save the HTML document and script file, then open the web page in a browser. Check the checkboxes, then call the context menu command to clear them all

The new features in this example were not fully supported in all web browsers at the time of publication. The Firefox browser was the first to introduce support, and produced the results illustrated here.

Dragging and dropping objects

The ability to allow the user to drag page objects and drop them onto a target is supported in HTML5 by the Drag and Drop API. This specifies many events that fire when the user drags an object but most important are the "dragstart", "dragover", and "drop" events. Event-handlers need to be scripted for each one of these events:

- **ondragstart event-handler** – to specify the Text data to be attached to the object being dragged, when dragging starts.

- **ondragover event-handler** – to cancel the default behavior of the drop target, thereby allowing objects to be dropped on it.

- **ondrop event-handler** – to define what should happen when an object gets dropped on the drop target.

Additionally, the ondrop event-handler should typically ensure that the target cannot be dropped on itself:

dragndrop.html

1 Create an HTML5 document that incorporates a script, and includes drag and drop images in the body section, along with an empty list

```
<script src="dragndrop.js"> </script>

<img id="bin" src="bin.png">
<img id="Red" src="red.png">
<img id="Yellow" src="yel.png">
<img id="Green" src="grn.png">
<fieldset><legend>Folders Dropped:</legend>
<ol id="msg" ></ol></fieldset>
```

dragndrop.js

2 Next, create a script that gets a reference for each image and the list when the HTML document has loaded

```
function init()
{
  var bin = document.getElementById( "bin" ) ;
  var gfx = document.getElementsByTagName( "img" ) ;
  var msg = document.getElementById( "msg" ) ;
  /*  More instructions go here */
}
onload = init ;
```

3 For the ondragstart event-handler, add a loop to attach the **id** of the image element being dragged as Text data

```
for( var i = 0 ; i < gfx.length ; i++ )
{
  gfx[ i ].ondragstart = function( event )
  { event.dataTransfer.setData( "Text", this.id ) ; } ;
}
```

Notice that the arguments to the dragstart event's **dataTransfer.setData()** method specify the data format and the actual data – in this case, the "Text" format and the **id** of the dragged element.

4 For the ondragover event-handler, cancel the default behavior of the bin – so objects can be dropped on it

```
bin.ondragover = function( event ) { return false ; } ;
```

5 For the ondrop event-handler, first get the **id** of the object being dropped and a reference for that image element

```
bin.ondrop = function( event )
{
  var did = event.dataTransfer.getData( "Text" ) ;
  var tag = document.getElementById( did ) ;
  /* More instructions go here */
} ;
```

6 Next, insert an instruction to write the **id** of the dropped element into the list – unless it is the bin image itself

```
if( did === "bin" ) { return false ; }
else { msg.innerHTML += "<li>"+did+"</li>" ; }
```

7 Finally, insert instructions to remove the dropped image element from the page, and to end the drop function

```
tag.parentNode.removeChild( tag ) ;  return false ;
```

The efficiency of the Drag and Drop API is the subject of some controversy, so it may be subject to revision.

8 Save the HTML document and script, then open the web page in your browser – drag and drop the folders on the bin

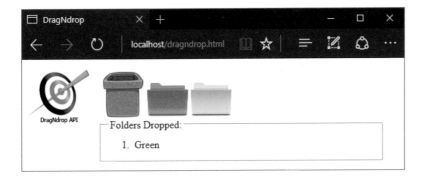

Manipulating pixels

The Canvas 2D API is part of the HTML5 specifications. Find details at w3.org/ TR/2dcontext

The amazing ability to manipulate the color of pixels in an image is provided in HTML5 by the Canvas 2D API, which was introduced in the previous chapter (Chapter Nine). The canvas context object has a **drawImage()** method that can copy a specified image onto a canvas, at specified XY coordinates. Information describing the color of each pixel on the canvas can then be stored in a "CanvasPixelArray" using the context object's **getImageData()** method. This method requires four arguments to specify the XY coordinates, width, and height of the area to be stored.

A CanvasPixelArray object has **width**, **height** and **data** properties. Of most interest, the **data** property is an array of the red, green, blue, and alpha components of each pixel stored in sequence. For example, with [r1, g1, b1, a1, r2, g2, b2, a2, r3, g3, b3, a3], the array elements r1, g1, b1, a1 describe the red, green, blue, and alpha components of the very first pixel – giving each color a numerical value in the range 0-255. Manipulating the numerical value in the array modifies the stored image data. The modified image can then be painted back onto the canvas, using the context object's **putImageData()** method to specify the array name, and the XY coordinates on the canvas at which to paint the image:

pixel.html

1 Create an HTML5 document that incorporates a script, and in the body section includes a single image and a canvas – both of the same size

```
<script src="pixel.js"> </script>

<img id="pixel" src="pixel.png"
        width="215" height="150" alt="Blue Flag" >
<canvas id="canvas" width="215" height="150" >
[Fallback Message]</canvas>
```

pixel.js

2 Now, create a script to copy the image onto the canvas when the document has loaded

```
function init()
{
  var canvas = document.getElementById( "canvas" ) ;
  if ( canvas.getContext )
  {
    var ctx = canvas.getContext( "2d" ) ;
    var img = document.getElementById( "pixel" ) ;
    ctx.drawImage( img, 0, 0 ) ;
    /* More instructions go here */
  }
} onload = init ;
```

3 Next, insert an instruction to read all pixels from the canvas into a pixel array
```
var pixels =
        ctx.getImageData( 0, 0, img.width, img.height ) ;
```

4 Then, insert a loop construct to iterate through each RGBA alpha component of the pixel array
```
for ( var i = 3 ; i < pixels.data.length ; i +=4 )
{
  /* More instructions go here */
}
```

Hot tip

White has an RGB color value of 255,255,255 so the script tests each green color component for the value 255 to identify each white pixel.

5 In the loop construct, insert instructions to ignore white pixels but change all blue pixels to red
```
if ( pixels.data[ i-2 ] !== 255 )
  {
    pixels.data[ i-1 ] = 0 ;        // Set b=0 – remove blue
    pixels.data[ i-3 ] =255 ;       // Set r=255 – make red
  }
```

6 Finally, insert an instruction to paint the manipulated pixel array onto the canvas
```
ctx.putImageData( pixels, 0, 0 ) ;
```

7 Save the HTML document and script, then open the web page in your browser, via a web server, to see the modified image painted onto the canvas

Beware

To use this technique, the source image for the **drawImage()** method must be served via the HTTP protocol from a web server (not a local file system), and it must be located on the same domain as the HTML document.

Storing user data

The Web Storage API is part of the HTML5 specifications. Find details at w3.org/TR/webstorage

The ability to store user data is supported in HTML5 by the excellent Web Storage API that makes storing user data a breeze. This provides a **localStorage** object, which retains stored data even after the browser has been closed, and the **sessionStorage** object, which retains stored data only until the browser gets closed. Each of these objects has identical methods to store and retrieve data.

The **setItem()** method requires two arguments to specify a key, and the data to be stored. For example, using the key "Name" in **localStorage.setItem("Name", "Mike")**. Stored data can then be retrieved, by specifying the key as the sole argument to the **getItem()** method, or removed by specifying the key as the sole argument to a **removeItem()** method. Additionally, all stored items can be deleted using the **clear()** method – without any arguments.

1 Create an HTML5 document that incorporates a script, and in the body section includes a fieldset containing a text input and three buttons

local.html

```
<script src = "local.js" > </script>

<fieldset><legend id = "leg" >Enter Name</legend>
<input type = "text" id = "username" >
<button onclick="storeName()">Store Name</button>
<button onclick="recallName()">Recall Name</button>
<button onclick="removeName()">Remove Name</button>
</fieldset>
```

local.js

2 Now, create a script with an event-handler function for the first button – to save the user data in local storage if valid

```
function storeName()
{
  var username =
        document.getElementById("username").value ;
  if( username === "null" || username === "" ) return false;
  localStorage.setItem( "user", username ) ;
   /* More instructions go here */
}
```

Backstroke characters in this script simply escape some quote marks.

3 Next, in the script function, insert instructions to clear the text field and display a confirmation message

```
document.getElementById( "username" ).value = "" ;
document.getElementById("leg").innerHTML =
"\""+ localStorage.getItem("user") + "\" is Stored";
```

4 Add an event-handler function for the second button – to retrieve and display the user data in local storage

```
function recallName()
{
  if( localStorage.getItem("user") === null ) return false ;
  document.getElementById( "username" ).value = "" ;
  document.getElementById("leg").innerHTML =
  "Stored Name is \""+ localStorage.getItem("user") + "\"" ;
}
```

5 Finally, add an event-handler function for the third button – to remove the user data in local storage

```
function removeName()
{
  if( localStorage.getItem("user") === null ) return false ;
  document.getElementById("leg").innerHTML =
  "\"" + localStorage.getItem("user") + "\" is Removed" ;
  localStorage.removeItem("user") ;
  document.getElementById( "username" ).value = "" ;
}
```

Hot tip

A shorthand alternative lets you simply tag the key onto the object name. For example, **localStorage. setItem("A","1")** can be expressed as **localStorage.A="1"** and **localStorage. getItem("A")** as **localStorage.A**.

6 Save the HTML document and script, then open the web page in your browser and store user name data

Beware

All data in **localStorage** and **sessionStorage** is stored as string values – so attempting to add retrieved values of 5 and 7 will get concatenated as 57, not totaled to 12.

7 Restart your browser and reopen this page, then push "Recall Name" to see the user data has been retained

Don't forget

Push the "Remove Name" button to delete data from local storage.

Editing live content

The Web Storage API, introduced in the previous example on pages 202-203, makes storing user data in HTML5 so much easier than the old method of setting "cookies". Restrictions allow only 20 cookies per domain, and limit the amount of text data they can each store to 4KB – allowing a maximum total of (20 x 4) 80 Kilobytes per domain. By stark contrast, Web Storage allows over 5 Megabytes per domain.

The **localStorage** object, which retains user data after the browser gets closed, is useful to store constant user data – such as user names and passwords. The **sessionStorage** object, which releases user data after the browser gets closed, is useful to store transient user data – such as the items in a shopping session basket.

The content of any page element can be made editable, so the user can modify its content, by adding a global **contenteditable** attribute to the element. The modified content can then be stored by **sessionStorage** to be temporarily available until the user closes the browser, thereby ending the session:

session.html

session.js

1. Create an HTML5 document that incorporates a script, and in the body section include an editable list and three buttons – to store and retrieve session data

```
<script src = "session.js" > </script>

<ul contenteditable="true" id="list">
            <li>Red<li>Green<li>Blue</ul>

<button id="restore" onclick="restore()">
        Restore Original List</button>

<button id="show" onclick="show()">
        Restore My List</button>

<button id="wipe" onclick="wipe()">
        Delete My List</button>
```

2. Now, create a script with a function to store the original list items as soon as the HTML document has loaded

```
function init()
{
  sessionStorage.setItem( "originalList" ,
      document.getElementById( "list").innerHTML ) ;
}
onload = init ;
```

...cont'd

3 Next, add an event-handler function for the first button – to store the edited list, then display the original list

```
function restore() {
 sessionStorage.setItem( "customList" ,
        document.getElementById( "list" ).innerHTML ) ;
document.getElementById( "list" ).innerHTML =
            sessionStorage.getItem( "originalList" ) ;
}
```

4 Now, add an event-handler function for the second button – to simply display the stored edited list

```
function show() {
 document.getElementById( "list" ).innerHTML =
            sessionStorage.getItem( "customList" );
}
```

5 Add an event-handler function for the third button – to display the original list, then remove the stored edited list

```
function wipe() {
 document.getElementById( "list" ).innerHTML =
            sessionStorage.getItem( "originalList" ) ;
 sessionStorage.removeItem( "customList" ) ;
}
```

6 Save the HTML document and script, then open the web page, edit the list, and use the buttons for session storage

If you want an entire document to be editable, you can simply include the script instruction **document.designMode ="on";** (notice that's "**on**" not "**true**") in the **init()** function – much easier than adding lots of **contenteditable** attributes.

Items in session storage remain available even when the user navigates to a different domain, then returns. They are only lost when the browser gets closed.

Cross-document messaging

The ability to allow plain text messages to be securely sent between documents is supported in HTML5 by the Web Messaging API. This is even possible when the documents are hosted on two different domains. For example, a document hosted on the local domain might include an inline frame containing a document from a different domain, which can securely send messages to each other.

To send a message to another document, a reference to the receiving document's containing window is first required by the sending document. For an inline frame, this is available from its **contentWindow** property. The Web Messaging API then provides it a **postMessage()** method that requires two arguments – to specify the message to be sent, and the target document domain. For example, **otherWindow.postMessage("Hello", "http://example.com")**.

In order to receive a message sent from another document, a message "listener" must first be added to the receiving document. This requires three arguments be supplied to that window's **addEventListener()** method – to specify it should listen for a "message" type, the event-handler function to process the message, and a Boolean **false** value to indicate no further processing is required.

The message is passed to the event-handler as an "event" that has an **origin** property, containing the domain of the sending document, and a **data** property, containing the text message.

The Web Messaging API is part of the HTML5 specifications. Find details at **w3.org/TR/webmessaging**

1 Create an HTML5 document that incorporates a script, a paragraph to display the document domain, an inline frame for a remote domain, and a "Send Message" button

```
<script src = "http://localhost/msg.js" > </script>

<p id = "host" >Main Page Domain: </p>
<iframe id = "ifr" width = "350" height = "120"
  src= "http://ineasysteps.com/msg-receive.html" >
</iframe>
<button onclick = "sendMsg()" >Send Message</button>
```

msg-send.html

2 Next, create an HTML document that incorporates the same script and has paragraphs to display the domain and message

```
<script src = "http://localhost/msg.js" > </script>

<p id = "host">Iframe Page Domain: </p>
<p id = "para" ></p>
```

msg-receive.html

③ Now, create the script to send and receive a message

```
function init() {
  document.getElementById("host").innerHTML +=
                           document.domain ;
  addEventListener( "message", readMsg, false ) ;
} onload = init ;

function sendMsg() {
  var win=document.getElementById("ifr").contentWindow ;
  win.postMessage( "Message Received from: " +
  document.domain, "http://ineasysteps.com" ) ;
}

function readMsg(event)  {
  if ( event.origin === "http://localhost" )
  document.getElementById("para").innerHTML=( event.data );
}
```

④ Save the first HTML document and script on the local domain, and the second HTML document on the remote domain, then click to send a cross-document message

msg.js

Hot tip

The HTML documents need not share the same script, but as they do, **msg-send.html** is already listening for messages – so this example could be extended to allow it to receive messages sent from **msg-receive.html**.

Don't forget

As a security precaution, cross-document messaging only succeeds when the sender correctly specifies the receiver's domain in the **postMessage()** method, and the receiver correctly verifies the sender's domain in the message's **event.origin** property.

Pinpointing the user

The ability to pinpoint the user's geographic location is supported in HTML5 by the wonderful Geolocation API. This first requests the user's consent to share location details – to send information about nearby wireless access points and the computer's IP address to, say, Google Location Services. This service returns the user's estimated latitude and longitude coordinates. Coordinates successfully retrieved can be displayed on the page, and supplied to the Google Maps service to acquire a map at that location:

geo.html

geo.js

The Geolocation API is not strictly part of the HTML5 specification. You can find details online at **dev.w3.org/geo/api**

1 Create an HTML document that incorporates two scripts, and includes two empty paragraphs in the body section
```
<script src = "geo.js" > </script>
<script src =
  "http://maps.google.com/maps/api/js?sensor=false">
</script>
<p id = "msg" ></p> <p id = "map" ></p>
```

2 Now, create a script with a function that attempts to seek the user location when the HTML document has loaded
```
function init()
{
  if ( navigator.geolocation )
  { document.getElementById( "msg" ).innerHTML =
        "Geolocation service is trying to find you...";
    navigator.geolocation.getCurrentPosition
        ( successFunction, errorFunction ) ; }
  else { document.getElementById( "msg" ).innerHTML =
  "Your browser does not support Geolocation service" ; }
} onload = init ;
```

3 Next, add a function to display a message if the attempt fails
```
function errorFunction( position )
{  document.getElementById( "msg" ).innerHTML =
   "Geolocation service cannot find you at this time." ; }
```

4 Add a success function to display the retrieved coordinates when the attempt succeeds
```
function successFunction( position )
{
  var lat = position.coords.latitude ;
  var lng = position.coords.longitude ;
  document.getElementById( "msg" ).innerHTML =
  "Found you at...<br>Latitude: "+lat+", Longitude: "+lng ;
  /* More instructions go here */
}
```

5 Now, in the success function, add instructions to load a map from Google Maps – using the retrieved coordinates

```
var latlng = new google.maps.LatLng( lat, lng ) ;
var options = { zoom: 18, center : latlng,
        mapTypeId: google.maps.MapTypeId.ROADMAP } ;
var map = new google.maps.Map
        ( document.getElementById( "map" ), options ) ;
var marker = new google.maps.Marker(
        { position: latlng, map: map, title:"You are here" } ) ;
```

6 Save the HTML document and script, then open the web page – agree to share your location to get pinpointed

In this example, the **navigator.geolocation** object provides the **getCurrentPosition()** method that must specify functions to handle success and failure. These functions must each accept a returned **position** object argument, as that contains the coordinates or error details.

209

You can supply any coordinates to the **lat** and **lng** variables to see a map at that location.

HTML5's native Drag and Drop capability, enhanced Web Storage for user data, secure cross-document Web Messaging between domains, and Geolocation services, present fantastic exciting possibilities – and more great APIs will be added in the future.

Summary

- The fundamental Application Programming Interface (API) available in any HTML document is provided by the Document Object Model (DOM).

- Each element and attribute within a document is represented as a DOM object that can be manipulated by script.

- The **<details>** and **<summary>** elements can respond to user actions without scripting.

- Context menu commands can be specified using the interactive **<menu>** and **<menuitem>** elements.

- The **<meter>** tag should contain a **value** attribute to define a measurement in a range specified to its **min** and **max** attributes.

- The Drag and Drop API allows the user to drag page objects and drop them onto a target within the page – by scripting **ondragstart, ondragover,** and **ondrop** event-handler functions.

- The Canvas 2D API can be used to manipulate pixel color via the **data** property of its CanvasPixelArray object.

- The Web Storage API provides the ability to store user data – either permanently with its **localStorage** object, or temporarily until the browser gets closed with its **sessionStorage** object.

- The Web Messaging API allows plain text messages to be sent securely between documents with its **postMessage()** method – and the documents need not be on the same domain.

- The Geolocation API provides the ability to pinpoint the user's location by estimating latitude and longitude coordinates – but only if the user consents to send information.

Handy reference

This section of the book lists **212** Global HTML5 attributes

and describes HTML5 **214** HTML5 element tags

elements and attributes. **232** CSS properties & values

Global HTML5 attributes

The attributes in the table below may each be included in any HTML5 element, so are therefore known as "global" attributes.

The **dropzone** attribute is a new global attribute introduced in HTML 5.1.

A comprehensive list of standard language abbreviations is maintained by the Internet Assigned Numbers Authority (IANA), and can be found online at iana.org/ assignments/language-subtag-registry

Attribute:	Specifies:
accesskey	A keyboard shortcut key Example: **accesskey="A"**
class	One or more space-separated class names Example: **class="recipes fish"**
contenteditable	An area where the user may edit content Example: **contenteditable="true"**
dir	Text direction **ltr** (left-to-right) or **rtl** Example: **dir="rtl"**
draggable	Element may be dragged and dropped Example: **draggable="true"**
dropzone	Action to perform by a drop target Example: **dropzone="copy file:image/png"**
hidden	Relevance to displayed content Example: **hidden="true"**
id	Unique identity name for the element Example: **id="item_22"**
lang	Content language by standard abbreviation Example: **lang="fr"** (French)
spellcheck	Whether content spelling can be checked Example: **spellcheck="true"**
style	One or more CSS style rules Example: **style="border:2px solid red;"**
tabindex	Sequential position using the Tab key Example: **tabindex="3"**
title	Advisory information such as a tooltip Example: **title="This item is draggable"**
translate	Whether content language can be translated when the page is localized Example: **translate="yes"**

In addition to those global attributes in the table opposite, the following global attributes in the table below may also be included in any HTML5 element. These attributes each allow a specified script function to be called when a particular event occurs on the element, so are therefore known as "event-handler" attributes.

onabort	onblur	oncancel
oncanplay	oncanplaythrough	onchange
onclick	onclose †	oncontextmenu †
oncopy †	oncuechange	oncut †
ondblclick	ondrag †	ondragend †
ondragenter †	ondragexit †	ondragleave †
ondragover †	ondragstart †	ondrop †
ondurationchange	onemptied	onended
onerror	onfocus	oninput
oninvalid	onkeydown	onkeypress
onkeyup	onload	onloadeddata
onloadedmetadata	onloadstart	onmousedown
onmouseenter	onmouseleave	onmousemove
onmouseout	onmouseover	onmouseup
onpaste	onpause	onplay
onplaying	onprogress	onratechange
onreset	onresize	onscroll
onseeked	onseeking	onselect
onshow	onstalled	onsubmit
onsuspend	ontimeupdate	ontoggle
onvolumechange	onwaiting	onwheel

Attributes marked with a † symbol, such as those relating to Drag and Drop, are new global attributes introduced in HTML 5.1.

Although all these attributes can be used in any HTML5 element, they are not necessarily useful in all elements.

HTML5 element tags

The following tables describe HTML5 element tags, together with their element-specific attributes. These attributes may be included within the associated tag, in addition to the global attributes and event-handler attributes described on pages 212-213.

Don't forget

HTML5 tags are NOT case-sensitive, so may appear as uppercase or lowercase characters.

Element:	Description:
<!-- -->	Comment tag. Encloses text comments that are ignored by the browser. Empty element – no closing tag required
Attributes:	None
<!DOCTYPE>	Document type declaration tag. The very first element in each document, defining the HTML markup version being used. Empty element – no closing tag required
Attributes:	**HTML** – Required to identify the markup version as HTML5 and so set the browser to Standards Mode
<a>	Anchor tag. Encloses a hyperlink, or acts as a placeholder
Attributes:	**href** – States the URL of a hyperlink target Or when used to specify a placeholder... **target** – Specifies a context name **hreflang** – Advises of the target language **media** – Advises of the target media **rel** – Advises of the target relationship **type** – Advises of the target MIME type
<abbr>	Abbreviation tag. Encloses an abbreviation
Attributes:	**title** – (global attribute) can be included to specify an expansion of the abbreviation
<address>	Address tag. Encloses contact information
Attributes:	None

Element:	Description:
<area>	Area tag. Specifies an area of an image map defined by its attributes. Empty element – no closing tag required
Attributes:	**alt** – Specifies alternative text like a tooltip **shape** – Defines the area shape **coords** – States the area's XY coordinates **href** – States the URL of a hyperlink target **hreflang** – Specifies language of resource **target** – Specifies a context name **media** – Advises of the target media **rel** – Advises of the target relationship **download** – Specifies resource file name **type** – Specifies the resource type
<article>	Article tag. Encloses a self-contained composition within a page
Attributes:	None
<aside>	Aside tag. Encloses content related to the adjacent content, such as in a sidebar
Attributes:	None
<audio>	Audio tag. Encloses source elements and specifies audio media content
Attributes:	**src** – States the URL of the audio resource **preload** – Advises of play likelihood **autoplay** – Specifies automatic play **loop** – Specifies automatic replay **controls** – Provides user interface controls **muted** – Whether muted by default **crossorigin** – How to share the resource
<b>	Bold tag. Encloses content that is to be displayed in a bold font
Attributes:	None
<base>	Base tag. Specifies a default address or a default target for all links on a page Empty element – no closing tag required
Attributes:	**href** – States the URL of a hyperlink target **target** – Specifies a context name

Beware

215

Web browsers support different codecs for audio playback, so it is recommended the **<audio>** tag be used to enclose **<source>** tags that specify alternative audio formats.

...element tags cont'd

Element:	Description:
\<bdi>	Bi-Directional Isolation tag. Encloses text written in a different direction to other text
\<bdo>	Bi-Directional Override tag. Encloses text to be written in a specific direction
Attributes:	**dir** – Specifies text direction as either "rtl" (right-to-left) or "ltr" (left-to-right)
\<blockquote>	Blockquote tag. Encloses a long quotation, typically automatically inset from preceding content
Attributes:	**cite** – Specifies a URL where the origin of the quotation is available
\<body>	Body tag. Encloses the entire contents of the document including text, hyperlinks, images, tables, lists, audio, video, etc.
Attributes:	**onload**, **onunload** – (global attributes) Specifies script to run when the document loads or unloads **onbeforeunload** – Specifies script to run before the document unloads **onbeforeprint**, **onafterprint** – Specifies script to run before and after print preview **onhashchange** – Specifies script to run when following a link within the page **onoffline**, **ononline** – Specifies script to run when connection is lost and restored **onmessage** – Specifies script to run when the user sends a cross-document message **onresize** – Specifies script to run when the browser window size gets changed **onpagehide**, **onpageshow** – Specifies script to run when page is hidden or restored **onpopstate** – Specifies script to run when the browser history changes **onstorage** – Specifies script to run when the Web Storage area changes **onrejectionhandled**, **onunhandledrejection** – Specifies script to run upon rejection

The global attributes **onblur**, **onerror**, **onfocus**, and **onload** each specify event-handlers for the top-level window object when included within the **\<body>** tag.

The **onrejectionhandled**, **onunhandledrejection** attributes are new promise-tracking features introduced in the HTML 5.1 specifications.

216

Element:	Description:
**\ **	Break tag. Inserts a single line break Empty element – no closing tag required
Attributes:	None
\<button>	Button tag. Encloses text to appear on a user-activated button
Attributes:	**type** – Specifies whether the button has a "button", "submit", or "reset" action **name, value** – Specifies the element's name/value key pair for form submission **disabled** – Suppresses user interaction **autofocus** – Sets automatic focus **form** – Specifies associated **\<form>** element
\<canvas>	Canvas tag. Inserts an invisible area that can be drawn in by script
Attributes:	**width** – Specifies the area's width **height** – Specifies the area's height
\<caption>	Caption tag. Encloses a table caption
Attributes:	None
\<cite>	Citation tag. Encloses the title of a work, such as a book, film, or song
Attributes:	None
\<code>	Code tag. Encloses computer code text
Attributes:	None
\<col>	Column tag. Identifies one or more table columns within a column group Empty element – no closing tag required
Attributes:	**span** – Specifies the number of columns
\<colgroup>	Column group tag. Encloses **\<col>** tags, or specifies a number of columns
Attributes:	**span** – Specifies the number of columns
\<data>	Data tag. Encloses data content in a human-readable format
Attributes:	**value** – Specifies a machine-readable version of the element's content

A **\<button>** tag can also include **formaction**, **formenctype**, **formmethod**, **formtarget**, and **formnovalidate** attributes for submission of an associated form.

The **\<cite>** tag should not be used to enclose a person's name.

…element tags cont'd

The **<details>** tag is a new element introduced in HTML 5.1.

Element:	Description:
<datalist>	Data List tag. Encloses a set of pre-defined control **<option>** elements
Attributes:	None
<dd>	Definition-list Description tag. Encloses the description of a definition term within a definition list
Attributes:	None
<del>	Deleted tag. Encloses text that has been deleted from the document
Attributes:	**cite** – Specifies a URL where an explanation for the deletion is available **datetime** – Specifies the time and date when the deletion was made
<details>	Details tag. Encloses additional information or controls
Attributes:	**open** – Specifies whether the details are visible
<dfn>	Definitive tag. Specifies that the enclosed term is the defining instance of that term
Attributes:	**title** – (global attribute) Specifies the exact value of the term being defined
<div>	Division tag. Encloses a group of other elements for styling purposes only
Attributes:	None
<dl>	Definition List tag. Encloses definition description and definition term tags to create a definition list
Attributes:	None
<dt>	Definition Term tag. Encloses a definition term within a definition list
Attributes:	None
<em>	Emphasis tag. Encloses text that should be displayed in an emphasized manner
Attributes:	None

Element:	Description:
\<embed\>	Embed tag. Identifies a resource to be imported into the document Empty element – no closing tag required
Attributes:	**src** – Specifies the URL of a resource **type** – Specifies the resource MIME type **width, height** – Specifies the allocated width and height within the document
\<fieldset\>	Fieldset tag. Encloses related form elements to group them together
Attributes:	**name** – Specifies the element's name **form** – Specifies an associated form **disabled** – Suppresses user interaction
\<figure\>	Figure tag. Encloses related content such as illustrations and diagrams
Attributes:	None
\<figcaption\>	Figure Caption tag. Encloses a caption for its parent **\<figure\>** element
Attributes:	None
\<footer\>	Footer tag. Encloses text providing document information, such as author name, contact details, copyright, etc.
Attributes:	None
\<form\>	Form tag. Encloses one or more form control elements for user input, such as text fields, checkboxes, buttons, etc.
Attributes:	**autocomplete** – Specifies whether the input completion state is "on" or "off" **name** – Specifies a unique form name **action** – Specifies a URL to which the form data is sent upon form submission **method** – Specifies the submission method as "GET", "POST", "PUT" or "DELETE" **enctype** – Specifies the MIME type to be used to encode the form data **novalidate** – Bypasses a validation check **target** – States where to display response

The values specified by the **\<embed\>** tag's **width** and **height** attributes need not state the actual dimensions of the resource.

Typically, a document will have just one **\<header\>** element (at the start) and one **\<footer\>** element (at the end).

A **\<form\>** tag can also include an **accept-charset** attribute to specify the character encoding of a form.

...element tags cont'd

Element:	Description:
\<h1> \<h2> **\<h3> \<h4>** **\<h5> \<h6>**	Heading tags. Encloses text to appear as document or section headings, ranked by prominence where **\<h1>** has the highest rank and **\<h6>** has the lowest
Attributes:	None
\<head>	Head tag. Encloses elements that provide information about the document, such as title, meta data, scripts, stylesheets, etc.
Attributes:	None
\<header>	Header tag. Encloses a document introduction that typically includes a heading element or heading group
Attributes:	None
\<hr>	Horizontal Rule tag. Inserts a horizontal ruled line between differing content Empty element – no closing tag required
Attributes:	None
\<html>	HTML tag. Encloses the entire head and body sections of the document
Attributes:	None
\<i>	Italics tag. Encloses content that is to be displayed in an italic font
Attributes:	None
\<iframe>	Inline Frame tag. Inserts a inline framed area containing another document
Attributes:	**src** – Specifies the URL of the document to appear within the inline frame **srcdoc** – Specifies a document to appear within the inline frame **name** – Specifies a unique frame name **width** – Specifies the frame width **height** – Specifies the frame height **sandbox** – Specifies security rules **allowfullscreen** – Sets fullscreen permission

220

Hot tip

The top-level **\<html>** element is also known as the "root" element.

Element:	Description:
<img>	Image tag. Inserts an image into the document Empty element – no closing tag required
Attributes:	**src** – Specifies the URL of the image **alt** – Specifies a required alternative text description of the image **width** – Specifies the image width **height** – Specifies the image height **ismap** – States that the image is a server-side image map **usemap** – States that the image is a client-side image map **srcset** – Specifies alternative images **sizes** – Specifies size between breakpoints **crossorigin** – How to share the resource
<input>	Input tag. Inserts an interactive input field that allows the user to enter data Empty element – no closing tag required
Attributes:	**type** – Specifies the input type, such as "text", "radio", "checkbox", etc. **name** – Specifies a unique input name **value** – Specifies a default value for the input, such as a phrase in a text field **size** – Specifies how many characters can be visible in a text field **maxlength, minlength** – Specifies the number of permitted characters **readonly** – Prevents modification of a text field value by the user **multiple** – Allows multiple values **pattern** – Specifies a regular expression **autocomplete** – Specifies whether the input completion state is "on" or "off" **checked** – States that a checkbox or radio button should be initially checked **disabled** – Suppresses user interaction **required** – Specifies required completion **placeholder** – Specifies a user hint **min, max** – Specifies a permitted range

The values specified by the **<img>** tag's **width** and **height** attributes need not state the actual dimensions of the image.

The name and associated value of inputs are sent to a form's action URL upon form submission.

...element tags cont'd

Beware

The HTML 5.1 specifications also recognize an old **<keygen>** tag, but this is being removed so should no longer be used.

Element:	Description:
<ins>	Inserted tag. Encloses text that has been inserted into the document
Attributes:	**cite** – Specifies a URL where an explanation for the insertion is available **datetime** – Specifies the time and date when the insertion was made
<kbd>	Keyboard tag. Encloses text that is to be entered by the user from the keyboard
Attributes:	None
<label>	Label tag. Encloses text that is associated with an input element
Attributes:	**for** – Specifies the ID of the input element to which the text label is to be associated
<legend>	Legend tag. Encloses text that is a caption for a form fieldset
Attributes:	None
<li>	List Item tag. Encloses text that is an item in an unordered or ordered list
Attributes:	**value** – Specifies at which number in an ordered list to begin numbering
<link>	Link tag. Identifies a linked resource Empty element – no closing tag required
Attributes:	**rel** – Specifies the relationship between the document and the linked resource, such as "stylesheet", "icon", etc. **type** – Specifies the resource's MIME type **href** – Specifies the URL of the resource **hreflang** – Specifies the resource language **media** – Advises of the resource media **sizes** – Specifies linked icon dimensions **rev** – Specifies reverse relationship **crossorigin** – How to share the resource
<main>	Main tag. Encloses the main content area of the document
Attributes:	None

Element:	Description:
\<map>	Map tag. Encloses a number of area elements to define an image map
Attributes:	**name** – Specifies a unique map name
\<mark>	Mark tag. Encloses content highlighted for reference purposes
Attributes:	None
\<menu>	Menu tag. Encloses a group of commands
Attributes:	**type** – Specifies the type of menu **label** – Specifies the menu label text
\<menuitem>	Menu Item tag. Encloses a command that can be run from a popup menu
Attributes:	**type** – Specifies the type of command **label** – Specifies the command label text **icon** – Specifies a command icon **disabled** – Specifies whether disabled **checked** – Specifies whether checked **radiogroup** – Specifies a mutually exclusive group of commands **default** – Specifies the default command
\<meta>	Metadata tag. Specifies information about the document defined by its attributes Empty element – no closing tag required
Attributes:	**charset** – Specifies the character encoding used by the document, such as "UTF-8" **content** – Specifies information to be associated with an HTTP header or a name **http-equiv** – Specifies an HTTP header to be associated with the information assigned to the element's content attribute **name** – Specifies a name to be associated with the information assigned to the element's content attribute

Hot tip

An image-map is a single image with clickable areas that may each have different targets.

Don't forget

For the **\<menuitem>** tag, a **type="context"** attribute is intended to add a command to the right-click context menu.

...element tags cont'd

Element:		Description:
<meter>		Meter tag. Encloses a fractional value within a specified range
	Attributes:	**value** – Specifies the current value **min** – Specifies the lowest range boundary **max** – Specifies the upper range boundary **low** – Specifies the high limit of low range **high** – Specifies the low limit of high range **optimum** – Specifies the ideal range value
<nav>		Navigation tag. Encloses anchor elements that provide hyperlinks, to define a navigation section of the document
	Attributes:	None
<noscript>		No-Script tag. Encloses text to be displayed in the event that JavaScript is not enabled in the web browser
	Attributes:	None
<object>		Object tag. Inserts an object into the document
	Attributes:	**data** – Specifies the URL of the object **type** – Specifies the object's MIME type **name** – Specifies a unique object name **width** – Specifies the object width **height** – Specifies the object height **form** – Specifies an associated form **typemustmatch** – Requires the document Content-Type to match the resource type
<ol>		Ordered List tag. Encloses list item elements to define an ordered list
	Attributes:	**start** – Sets where to begin numbering **type** – Specifies the type of list marker **reversed** – Numbers in reverse order
<optgroup>		Option Group tag. Encloses related option elements in a drop-down selection list
	Attributes:	**label** – Specifies a required group name **disabled** – Suppresses user interaction

Hot tip

The **<object>** tag may also enclose text to be displayed in the event that the object cannot be inserted.

Element:	Description:
\<option\>	Option tag. Encloses text that is an item in a drop-down selection list
Attributes:	**value** – Specifies the value to be sent to the server if the item is selected **selected** – Sets the item selected by default **disabled** – Suppresses user interaction **label** – Specifies label text
\<output\>	Output tag. Encloses the result of a calculation or user action
Attributes:	**for** – Specifies the controls from which the output was calculated **form** – Specifies an associated form **name** – Specifies a name for submission
\<p\>	Paragraph tag. Encloses text and automatically adds space before and after itself to create a paragraph block
Attributes:	None
\<param\>	Parameter tag. Specifies runtime plug-in parameters for inserted objects Empty element – no closing tag required
Attributes:	**name** – [Required] Specifies a plug-in parameter name, such as "autoplay" **value** – [Required] Specifies a plug-in parameter value, such as "false"
\<picture\>	Picture tag. Encloses multiple **\<source\>** sources for an enclosed **\<img\>** element
Attributes:	None
\<pre\>	Preformatted tag. Encloses text that is to be displayed in a fixed-width font, preserving all spaces and line-breaks
Attributes:	None

Beware

The **\<p\>** element should not be used where a more meaningful element can be used.

225

...element tags cont'd

Element:	Description:
\<progress>	Progress tag. Encloses an indication of progress towards completion of a task
Attributes:	**value** – Specifies the current value **max** – Specifies the upper range boundary
\<q>	Quote tag. Encloses a short quotation, within automatically added quote marks
Attributes:	**cite** – Specifies a URL where the origin of the quotation is available
\<rb>	Ruby Base tag. Encloses the base text component of a ruby annotation
Attributes:	None
\<rp>	Ruby Parentheses tag. Encloses a parentheses character, which will be hidden in browsers that support ruby annotation
Attributes:	None
\<rt>	Ruby Text tag. Encloses a pronunciation explanation of text within a ruby element
Attributes:	None
\<rtc>	Ruby Text Container tag. Encloses the text components of a ruby annotation
Attributes:	None
\<ruby>	Ruby tag. Encloses text that requires a pronunciation explanation, along with ruby parentheses and ruby text elements
Attributes:	None
\<s>	Superseded tag. Encloses content that is no longer relevant
Attributes:	None
\<samp>	Sample tag. Encloses sample output from a computer program
Attributes:	None

The contents of a **\<samp>** element are typically displayed in a fixed-width font.

Element:	Description:
\<script\>	Script tag. Encloses script code, or specifies an external script resource
Attributes:	**type** – Specifies the script MIME type, such as "text/javascript" (the default) **src** – Specifies the URL of a script file **charset** – Specifies the character encoding used by the document, such as "UTF-8" **defer** – Specifies that the script may be processed after the page loads **async** – Executes the script in parallel **crossorigin** – How to share the resource
\<section\>	Section tag. Encloses text that is a section of a document, like a chapter
Attributes:	None
\<select\>	Selection tag. Encloses option elements to define a drop-down selection list
Attributes:	**name** – Specifies a unique list name **size** – Specifies the number of option items that may be visible in the list **multiple** – Specifies that more than one option item may be selected in the list **disabled** – Suppresses user interaction **autofocus** – Sets automatic focus **form** – Specifies an associated form **required** – Specifies required completion
\<small\>	Small print tag. Encloses text that is a side comment, such as a legal disclaimer
Attributes:	None
\<source\>	Source tag. Encloses optional fallback text and specifies a media resource, for audio and video elements
Attributes:	**src** – Specifies the URL of a media file **type** – Specifies the media's MIME type
\<span\>	Span tag. Encloses text for styling only
Attributes:	None

Don't forget

Both the **\<span\>** and **\<div\>** elements have no structural meaning, so are best avoided.

...element tags cont'd

Element:	Description:
\<strong>	Strong tag. Encloses text that should be considered to be important
Attributes:	None
\<style>	Style tag. Encloses style rules, to define a stylesheet
Attributes:	**type** – Specifies the stylesheet MIME type, such as "text/css" (the default) **media** – Specifies the intended viewing medium, such as "all" (the default)
\<sub>	Subscript tag. Encloses text that is to be displayed as subscript, such as in H_2O
Attributes:	None
\<summary>	Summary tag. Encloses a summary of the document body contents
Attributes:	None
\<sup>	Superscript tag. Encloses text that is to be displayed as superscript, such as in πr^2
Attributes:	None
\<table>	Table tag. Encloses table component elements, such the table header, footer, and body elements, to define a full table
Attributes:	**border** – Specifies borders may be drawn around cells with **border="1"**
\<tbody>	Table Body tag. Encloses table row and data elements, to define a table body
Attributes:	None
\<td>	Table Data tag. Encloses text data that is to be displayed in a regular table data cell
Attributes:	**colspan** – Specifies the number of columns the table data cell should span **rowspan** – Specifies the number of rows the table data cell should span **headers** – Specifies related header cells

The **\<summary>** tag is a new element introduced in HTML 5.1.

Element:	Description:
\<template\>	Template tag. Encloses fragments of HTML that may be cloned by scripting
Attributes:	None
\<textarea\>	Text Area tag. Encloses text within a multi-line text input field
Attributes:	**cols** – Specifies the number of characters per line, defining the area width **rows** – Specifies the number of visible rows, defining the area height **readonly** – Prevents modification of the text area content by the user **name** – Specifies a name for the text area **disabled** – Suppresses user interaction **autocomplete** – Specifies autofill hint **autofocus** – Sets automatic focus **dirname** – Specifies form field to submit for element directionality, either ltr or rtl **form** – Specifies an associated form **inputmode** – Specifies hint to select mode **minlength, maxlength** – Specifies the permissible number of characters **placeholder** – Specifies a user hint **required** – Specifies required completion **wrap** – Specifies how to wrap the text
\<tfoot\>	Table Footer tag. Encloses table row elements to define a table footer section
Attributes:	None
\<th\>	Table Heading tag. Encloses text that is to be displayed as a column heading
Attributes:	**colspan** – Specifies the number of columns the heading cell should span **rowspan** – Specifies the number of rows the heading cell should span **headers** – Specifies related header cells **scope** – Specifies related table **\<td\>** cells **abbr** – Specifies an alternative label by which to reference the **\<th\>** cell

...element tags cont'd

Beware

Don't confuse the **<th>** table heading elements, which define column headings, with the **<thead>** table header elements that define the entire table head section.

Element:	Description:
<thead>	Table Header tag. Encloses table row elements to define a table header section
Attributes:	None
<time>	Time tag. Encloses date and/or time content in a human-readable format
Attributes:	**datetime** – Specifies a machine-readable version of the element's content
<title>	Title tag. Encloses text that is the title of the HTML document
Attributes:	None
<tr>	Table Row tag. Encloses table data cell elements, to define an entire table row
Attributes:	None
<track>	Track tag. Encloses nothing, but its attributes provide subtitles for video
Attributes:	**kind** – Specifies the type of text track **src** – Specifies the URL of the resource **srclang** – Specifies the language of the text track **label** – Specifies the text of a label **default** – Specifies the default text track
<u>	Underline tag. Encloses misspelled text or a proper name in Chinese text
Attributes:	None
<ul>	Unordered List tag. Encloses list item elements to define an unordered list
Attributes:	None
<var>	Variable tag. Encloses text that is a mathematical or programming variable
Attributes:	None

Hot tip

The **<u>** element should generally be avoided, as underlined text indicates a hyperlink in HTML documents.

Element:	Description:
<video>	Video tag. Encloses source elements and specifies video media content
Attributes:	**src** – States the URL of the video resource **preload** – Advises how much buffering is likely to be needed **autoplay** – Specifies automatic playback **loop** – Specifies automatic replay **controls** – Provides user interface controls **width** – Specifies the video player width **height** – Specifies the video player height **crossorigin** – How to share the resource **poster** – Specifies the URL of an image to display before playback begins **muted** – Whether muted by default
<wbr>	Word Break tag. Encloses nothing, but denotes a line word-break opportunity
Attributes:	None

CSS properties & values

Many of the properties used in CSS style rules are listed in the table below. Size values can be specified as pixels with a **px** suffix, and colors can be specified as hexadecimal values in the range **#000000** to **#FFFFFF**, or by one of the pre-defined listed names.

Three-figure hexadecimal shorthand values can also be used for color values. For example, **#0F8** for **#00FF88**.

Property:	Example values:	Specifies:
margin	5px | 10% | auto	margin size
padding	5px | 10%	padding size
border	3px solid black	border size, type, and color
display	block | inline	level type
width	5px | 10%	width
height	5px | 10%	height
position	absolute | relative	positioning scheme
top	5px | 10%	distance from top
left	5px | 10%	distance from left
visibility	visible | hidden	show/hide element
overflow	visible | hidden	show/hide overflow
color	red | #FF0000	foreground color
background	white | url(tile.png)	background color or background image
font	large "Arial", sans-serif	font size and name
cursor	pointer | default	cursor type
text-align	center | left	inner text alignment

CSS provides many more properties than those listed here. More comprehensive information is available in the companion book in this series entitled *CSS3 in easy steps*.

Black	#000000	Green	#008000
Silver	#C0C0C0	Lime	#00FF00
Gray	#808080	Olive	#808000
White	#FFFFFF	Yellow	#FFFF00
Maroon	#800000	Navy	#000080
Red	#FF0000	Teal	#008080
Purple	#800080	Aqua	#00FFFF
Fuchsia	#FF00FF	Blue	#0000FF

Index

A

a, anchor element	66, 214
abbr, abbreviation element	58, 214
abbr, attribute (th)	229
absolute address	12
Abyss Personal Edition web server	144
accept-charset, attribute (form)	219
accesskey, attribute	68, 212
action, attribute (form)	144, 219
addColorStop(), context object method	180
addEventListener(), window method	206
address, element	92, 214
Advanced Audio Coding (AAC) codec	136
Advanced Video Coding (AVC) codec	138
advisory elements	
abbr, cite, dfn, kbd	58
allowfullscreen, attribute (iframe)	220
alt, alternative attribute (area)	76, 215
alt, alternative attribute (image button)	162
alt, alternative attribute (img)	60, 221
animation (canvas)	192
arc(), context object method	176, 186
area, element	76, 215
article, element	11, 88, 215
aside, element	11, 90, 215
async, attribute (script)	227
audio, element	11, 136, 215
autocomplete, attribute (form)	219
autocomplete, attribute (input)	221
autocomplete, attribute (textarea)	229
autofocus, attribute (button)	217
autofocus, attribute (select)	227
autofocus, attribute (textarea)	229
autoplay, attribute (audio)	136, 215
autoplay, attribute (video)	138, 231

B

base, element	36, 215
b, bold element	46, 215
bdi, bi-directional isolation element	62, 216
bdo, bi-directional override element	62, 216
beginPath(), context object method	176, 184
bezierCurveTo(), context object method	186
blockquote, element	44, 216
body, element	15, 40, 216

bookmarks	24
border, attribute (table)	228
border-collapse, CSS property	115
border, CSS property (table)	115
br, line break element	42, 217
bullet point (ul)	
disc, circle, square, image, none	100
button, element	164, 217
button, input type	160
button logo	164
Byte Order Mark (BOM)	17

C

Canvas 2D API	11, 200
canvas, element	11, 174, 217
CanvasGradient object	180
CanvasPattern object	180
CanvasPixelArray object	200
CanvasRenderingContext2D object	174
capitalization, tag names	14
caption, table caption element	107, 217
Cascading Style Sheet (CSS)	34
properties & values	232
charset, character set attribute (meta)	16, 26, 223
charset, character set attribute (script)	227
checkbox input	152
checked, attribute (checkbox input)	152, 221
checked, attribute (menuitem)	223
cite, attribute (blockquote)	44, 216
cite, attribute (del)	218
cite, attribute (ins)	222
cite, attribute (q)	44, 226
cite, element	58, 217
class, attribute	212
clearRect(), context object method	174
clear(), storage method	202
click event	33, 160
clip(), context object method	190
cloned elements	120
closePath(), context object method	176
codec (coder-decoder)	136, 138
code, element	56, 217
colgroup, table column group element	116, 217
colors	232
cols, columns attribute (textarea)	150, 229
colspan, table column span attribute (td)	110, 228
colspan, table column span attribute (th)	229

col, table column element | 118, 217
comments tag, <!-- --> | 15, 214
computer code elements
   code, var, samp | 56
content, attribute (meta) | 30, 223
contenteditable, attribute | 204, 212
contentWindow property (iframe) | 206
controls, attribute (audio) | 136, 215
controls, attribute (video) | 138, 231
cookies | 204
coords, attribute (area) | 76, 215
createLinearGradient(), context object method | 180
createPattern(), context object method | 180
createRadialGradient(), context object method | 180
cross-document messaging | 206
crossorigin, attribute (audio) | 215
crossorigin, attribute (link) | 222
crossorigin, attribute (script) | 227
crossorigin, attribute (video) | 231

disabled, attribute (text input) | 146
div, division element | 96, 218
dl, definition list element | 104, 218
document outline | 83
document structure | 14, 94
document title | 24
document type declaration,
   <!DOCTYPE HTML> | 14, 214
domain, address | 12
Domain Name Server (DNS) | 13
download, attribute (area) | 215
draggable, attribute | 212
dragging & dropping
   dragstart, dragover, drop, events | 198
Drag and Drop API | 11, 198
drawImage(), context object method | 200
drop-down list | 156
drop-shadow effect (canvas) | 182
dropzone, attribute | 212
dt, definition term element | 104, 218

D

data, attribute (object) | 128, 224
data, element | 56, 217
datalist, element | 168, 218
data, messaging event property | 206
data property (CanvasPixelArray) | 200
dataTransfer.getData(), drag event method | 199
dataTransfer.setData(), drag event method | 199
datetime, attribute (del) | 218
datetime, attribute (ins) | 222
datetime, attribute (time) | 56, 230
datetime-local, input type | 148
dd, definition description element | 104, 218
default, attribute (menuitem) | 223
default, attribute (track) | 138, 230
defer, attribute (script) | 227
del, deleted element | 48, 218
description, name value | 30
details, element | 11, 196, 218
dfn, definitive instance element | 58, 218
dir, attribute (bdo & bdi) | 62, 216
dir, direction attribute | 212
dirname, attribute (textarea) | 229
disabled, attribute (button) | 217
disabled, attribute (fieldset) | 219
disabled, attribute (input) | 221
disabled, attribute (menuitem) | 223
disabled, attribute (optgroup) | 224
disabled, attribute (option) | 225
disabled, attribute (select) | 227
disabled, attribute (textarea) | 229

E

embedding
   applets | 130
   audio | 136
   frames | 132
   objects | 128
   plugin movies | 134
   video | 138
embed, element | 11, 134, 219
em, emphasis element | 46, 218
emphasizing elements
   b, i, strong, em | 46
encoding, document
   BIG5 | 26
   ISO-8859-1 | 26
   SHIFT-JIS | 26
   US-ASCII | 26
   UTF-8 | 16, 26
enctype, encoding type attribute (form) | 170, 219
entities
   • | 119
   < >   © ® ™ | 24
   ² ³ | 54
event-handler attributes
   onclick, onload, etc. | 213
event-handler function | 40
Expression Web editor | 20
eXtensible Markup Language (XML) | 10, 134

F

fallback text	128, 174
fieldset, element	152, 219
figcaption, figure caption element	11, 124, 219
figure, element	11, 124, 219
fill(), context object method	176
fillRect(), context object method	174, 176
fillStyle, context object property	174
fillText(), context object method	182
Firefox browser	20, 31
Flash movie, embedding	134
flow elements	44
formatting elements	
small, del, ins	48
font, context object property	182
footer, element	11, 92, 219
for, attribute (label)	166, 222
for, attribute (output)	158, 225
formaction, attribute (button)	217
form, attribute (button)	217
form, attribute (fieldset)	219
form, attribute (object)	224
form, attribute (output)	225
form, attribute (select)	227
form, attribute (textarea)	229
form, element	144, 170, 219
formenctype, attribute (button)	217
formmethod, attribute (button)	217
formnovalidate, attribute (button)	217
formtarget, attribute (button)	217
fragment identifier	70

G

Geolocation API	208
getContext(), canvas method	174
getCurrentPosition(), geolocation method	209
getImageData(), context object method	200
getItem(), storage method	202
Google Chrome browser	20, 151
Google Location Services	208
Google Maps service	208

H

hash character, (a)	70
hash character (color value)	180
hash character (image map)	76
head, element	15, 220
header, element	11, 84, 220
headers, attribute (th)	229
headings	
grouping	84
h1 element	17
h1, h2, h3, h4, h5, h6, elements	82, 220
height, attribute (canvas)	174
height, attribute (embed)	134, 219
height, attribute (iframe)	132, 220
height, attribute (img)	60, 221
height, attribute (object)	128, 224
height, attribute (video)	138, 231
height, canvas property	217
height, property (CanvasPixelArray)	200
hidden, attribute	212
hidden input	158
high, attribute (meter)	224
history	24
href, attribute (a)	66, 70, 72, 78, 132, 214
href, attribute (area)	76, 215
href, attribute (base)	36, 215
href, attribute (link)	34, 222
hreflang, attribute (a)	214
hreflang, attribute (area)	215
hreflang, attribute (link)	222
hr, horizontal rule element	42, 220
HTML editor	20
html, element	15, 220
http-equiv, attribute (meta)	28, 223
HTTP headers	13
hyperlink	
accesskey	68
hover, active, visited, states	66
image map	76
images	74
page fragments	70
protocols	72
HyperText Markup Language (HTML)	10
HyperText Transfer Protocol (HTTP)	12

I

icon, attribute (menuitem)	223
icon resource, favicon.ico	36
id, identity attribute	70, 158, 166, 212
id, identity attribute (canvas)	174
id, identity attribute (output)	158
iframe, inline frame element	132, 206, 220
i, italic element	46, 220
image button input	162
images	
figure element	124
img, image element	60, 126, 162, 164, 221
img, image element (hyperlink)	74
img, image element (image map)	76
input, element	221
button	160
checkbox	152
file	170
hidden	158
image button	162
radio	154
submit	144
text	146
inputmode, attribute (textarea)	229
ins, inserted element	48, 222
IntelliSense	21
Internet Assigned Numbers Authority (IANA)	212
Internet Explorer browser	20
favicon.ico	36
Internet Protocol (IP) address	13
ismap, attribute (img)	221

J

Java applet	130
Java Runtime Environment (JRE)	130
JavaScript	11, 32

K

kbd, keyboard element	58, 222
keywords, name value	30
kind, attribute (track)	230

L

label, attribute (menu)	223
label, attribute (menuitem)	223
label, attribute (optgroup)	224
label, attribute (option)	225
label, attribute (track)	230
label, element (form controls)	166, 222
lang, attribute (html)	16
lang, language attribute	212
language elements	
bdo, bdi, ruby, rp, rt, rb, rtc	62
latitude and longitude coordinates	208
legend, element	152, 222
li, list item element	100, 102, 222
lineCap, context object property	184
lineJoin, context object property	184
lineTo(), context object method	176, 184
lineWidth, context object property	178, 184
link, element	34, 36, 222
list, attribute (input)	168
listener (events)	206
lists	
definition	104
ordered	102
unordered	100
list-style-image, CSS property	100
list-style-type, CSS property	100
load event	40
localhost, IP address (127.0.0.1)	144
localStorage object	202, 204
logos	164
loop, attribute (audio)	136, 215
loop, attribute (video)	138, 231
low, attribute (meter)	224

M

main, element	11, 94, 222
map, element	76, 223
mark, element	50, 223
Math.PI, JavaScript constant	176, 186
max, attribute (input)	221
max, attribute (meter)	196, 224
max, attribute (progress)	226
maxlength, attribute (textarea)	229
maxlength, attribute (text input)	146, 221
media, attribute (a)	214
media, attribute (area)	215
media, attribute (link)	222

media, attribute (style) 228
menu, element 11, 196, 223
menuitem, element 11, 196, 223
meta, element 16, 28, 30, 223
meter, element 196, 224
method, attribute (form) 144, 170, 219
Microsoft Edge browser 20
MIME type
    application/msword 128
    application/pdf 128
    application/x-java-applet 128
    application/x-shockwave-flash 134
    audio/mpeg 128
    audio/x-wav 128
    image/gif 128
    image/jpeg 128
    image/png 128
    image/svg+xml 128, 134
    text/css 34
    text/html 13, 128
    text/javascript 32
    text/plain 128
    video/mp4 128
    video/quicktime 128
    video/x-mpeg 128
    video/x-msvideo 128
    video/x-msv-wmv 128
min, attribute (input) 221
min, attribute (meter) 196, 224
minlength, attribute (input) 221
minlength, attribute (textarea) 229
miterLimit, context object property 184
modifying elements
    sub, sup 54
month, input type 148
moveTo(), context object method 176, 184
multiple, attribute (input) 221
multiple, attribute (select) 227
muted, attribute (audio) 215
muted, attribute (video) 231

N

name, attribute (button) 217
name, attribute (checkbox input) 152
name, attribute (fieldset) 219
name, attribute (file input) 170
name, attribute (form) 219
name, attribute (hidden input) 158
name, attribute (iframe) 132, 220
name, attribute (input) 221
name, attribute (map) 76, 223

name, attribute (meta) 30, 223
name, attribute (object) 224
name, attribute (output) 225
name, attribute (param) 130, 225
name, attribute (radio input) 152
name, attribute (select) 156, 227
name, attribute (submit input) 144
name, attribute (textarea) 150, 229
name, attribute (text input) 146
name=value pair 144
navigation tab 24
navigator.geolocation object 209
nav, navigation element 86, 224
new Image(), JavaScript constructor 180
noscript, element 32, 224
novalidate, attribute (form) 219
numbering type (ol)
    decimal, roman, latin, greek,
    georgian, armenian 102

O

object, element 128, 224
Ogg audio codec (vorbis) 136
Ogg video codec (theora) 138
ol, ordered list element 102, 224
onafterprint, attribute (body) 216
onbeforeprint, attribute (body) 216
onbeforeunload, attribute (body) 216
onclick, attribute 164
ondragover, attribute 198
ondragstart, attribute 198
ondrop, attribute 198
onhashchange, attribute (body) 216
oninput, attribute (form) 158
onload, attribute (body) 40, 216
onmessage, attribute (body) 216
onoffline, attribute (body) 216
ononline, attribute (body) 216
onpagehide, attribute (body) 216
onpageshow, attribute (body) 216
onpopstate, attribute (body) 216
onrejectionhandled, attribute (body) 216
onresize, attribute (body) 216
onstorage, attribute (body) 216
onunhandledrejection, attribute (body) 216
onunload, attribute (body) 216
open, attribute (details) 218
Opera browser 20
optgroup, option group element 224
optimum, attribute (meter) 224
option, element 156, 225

origin, messaging event property   206
outline   83
output, element   158, 225

P

param, parameter element   130, 225
parentNode.removeChild() method   199
password input   146
path, address   12
Perl, ActivePerl support   144
phrasing elements   44
picture, element   126, 225
pixel   200
pixelation   60
placeholder, attribute (input)   221
placeholder, attribute (textarea)   229
poly, attribute (map)   76
popup effect   78
Portable Document Format (PDF)   129
Portable Network Graphics (PNG)   60
positioning content   94
poster, attribute (video)   231
postMessage(), messaging method   206
p, paragraph element   42, 225
preload, attribute (audio)   136, 215
preload, attribute (video)   138, 231
pre, preformatted element   52, 225
progress, element   140, 226
protocols
    http: 12
    javascript: 72
    mailto: 72
pseudo-class (CSS)
    a:hover   78
pull-quotes   90
putImageData(), context object method   200

Q

q, quote element   44, 226
quadraticCurveTo(), context object method 186
quote marks (attributes)   40

R

radians   176, 186
radio button input   154
radiogroup, attribute (menuitem)   223
rb, ruby base element   62, 226
readonly, attribute (textarea)   150, 229
readonly, attribute (text input)   146, 221
rect, attribute (map)   76
refresh, http-equiv value   28
relative address   12
rel, attribute (a)   214
rel, relationship attribute (area)   215
rel, relationship attribute (link)   34, 222
    permitted values   36
removeItem(), storage method   202
required, attribute (input)   221
required, attribute (select)   227
required, attribute (textarea)   229
reset button   160, 164
response headers   151
restore(), context object method   188
rev, attribute (link)   36, 222
reversed, attribute (ol)   224
rgba() expression   180
rgb() expression   180
robots, name value   30
rollover effect   78
rotate(), context object method   188
rows, attribute (textarea)   150, 229
rowspan, table row span attribute (td) 108, 228
rowspan, table row span attribute (th)   229
rp, ruby parentheses element   11, 62, 226
rtc, ruby text container element   62, 226
rt, ruby text element   11, 62, 226
ruby annotation   62
ruby, element   11, 62, 226

S

Safari browser   20
samp, sample element   56, 226
sandbox, attribute (iframe)   220
save(), context object method   188
Scalable Vector Graphics (SVG)   134
scale(), context object method   188
scope, attribute (th)   229
script, element   32, 227
search engines   24
section, element   11, 88, 227

section limits	88
selected, attribute (option)	156, 225
select, element	156, 227
sessionStorage object	202, 204
setItem(), storage method	202
setTransform(), context object method	190
shadowBlur, context object property	182
shadowColor, context object property	182
shadowOffsetX, context object property	182
shadowOffsetY, context object property	182
shape, attribute (area)	76, 215
ShockWave Flash (SWF)	134
size, attribute (select)	156, 227
size, attribute (text input)	146, 221
sizes, attribute (link)	222
small, smallprint element	48, 92, 227
source, element (for audio/video)	11, 227
source, element (for picture)	126
span, attribute (col)	217
span, attribute (colgroup)	116, 217
span, element	96, 227
spellcheck, attribute	212
src, attribute (track)	138, 230
srcdoc, attribute (iframe)	220
srclang, attribute (track)	230
srcset, source set attribute (source)	126
src, source attribute (audio)	136, 215
src, source attribute (embed)	134, 219
src, source attribute (iframe)	132, 220
src, source attribute (img)	60, 221
src, source attribute (script)	32, 227
src, source attribute (source)	136, 227
src, source attribute (video)	138, 231
s, superseded element	50
start, attribute (ol)	102, 224
stroke(), context object method	178, 184
strokeRect(), context object method	178
strokeStyle, context object property	178, 184
strokeText(), context object method	182
strong, element	46, 228
structure	94
style, attribute	212
style, element	34, 228
style sheets	34
submission methods	
GET, POST	144, 150
submit button input	144, 164
sub, subscript element	54, 228
subtitles	138
summary, element	11, 196, 228
sup, superscript element	54, 228

tab characters	52
tabindex, attribute	166, 212
table, element	106, 228
target, attribute (a)	132, 214
target, attribute (area)	215
target, attribute (base)	215
target, attribute (form)	219
tbody, table body element	112, 228
td, table data element	106, 228
template, element	120, 229
text-align, CSS property	114
textarea, element	150, 229
Text-Art	52
text input	150
tfoot, table footer element	112, 229
thead, table header element	112, 230
th, table row/column heading element	107, 229
time, element	56, 230
title, attribute	58, 212
title, attribute (abbr)	214
title, attribute (dfn)	218
title bar	24
title, element	16, 24, 230
tooltips	58
track, element	138, 230
transformation matrix	190
transform(), context object method	190
translate, attribute	212
translate(), context object method	188
tr, table row element	106, 230
type, attribute (a)	214
type, attribute (area)	215
type, attribute (button element)	164, 217
type, attribute (button input)	160
type, attribute (checkbox input)	152
type, attribute (embed)	134, 219
type, attribute (file input)	170
type attribute (hidden input)	158
type, attribute (image button input)	162
type, attribute (input)	221
type, attribute (link)	34, 222
type, attribute (menu)	223
type, attribute (menuitem)	223
type, attribute (object)	130, 224
type, attribute (ol)	224
type, attribute (password input)	146
type, attribute (radio input)	154
type, attribute (script)	32, 227
type, attribute (source)	136, 138, 227
type, attribute (style)	228
type, attribute (submit input)	144

type, attribute (text input)   146
typemustmatch, attribute (object)   224

U

ul, unordered list element   100, 230
Unicode Transformation Format (UTF-8)   16
Uniform Resource Locator (URL)   12
uploading files   170
url, content property   28
usemap, attribute (img)   76, 221
usemap, attribute (object)   128
user data storage   202
u, underline element   50, 230

V

validating documents
    Compatibility Checker   21
    W3C Validator Tool   18
value, attribute (button)   217
value, attribute (checkbox input)   152
value, attribute (data)   56, 217
value, attribute (hidden input)   158
value, attribute (input)   221
value, attribute (li)   222
value, attribute (meter)   196, 224
value, attribute (option)   156, 225
value, attribute (param)   130, 225
value, attribute (progress)   226
value, attribute (radio input)   154
value, attribute (submit input)   144
value, attribute (text input)   146
var, code variable element   56, 230
vertical-align, CSS property   114
video, element   11, 138, 231

W

wbr, word-break element   50, 231
Web Messaging API   11, 206
Web Storage API   11, 202
Web Video Text Tracks (WebVTT)   138
week, input type   148
whitespace characters   15
width, attribute (canvas)   174
width, attribute (embed)   134, 219
width, attribute (iframe)   132, 220
width, attribute (img)   60, 221
width, attribute (object)   128, 224
width, attribute (video)   138, 231
width, canvas property   217
width, property (CanvasPixelArray)   200
World Wide Web Consortium (W3C)   10, 18
wrap, attribute (textarea)   229

X

XHTML (eXtensible HTML)   10
XML (eXtensible Markup Language)   10